# Agentic AI

A Practical Guide to Building Autonomous
Intelligent Systems

**Jude Max**

# Contents

# Introduction

The field of Artificial Intelligence stands at a pivotal juncture, transitioning from systems that primarily analyze and react to those that proactively reason, plan, and act with genuine autonomy. This transformative shift is embodied by **Agentic AI** – a powerful paradigm that empowers artificial entities to become intelligent agents, capable of independent decision-making and goal-directed behavior in complex, dynamic environments. Are you ready to move beyond the limitations of passive AI and embark on the journey of building truly intelligent systems that can shape our future?

"Agentic AI: A Practical Guide to Building Autonomous Intelligent Systems" serves as your comprehensive and accessible roadmap to this exciting frontier. This book is meticulously crafted to demystify the core principles and practical techniques required to design, develop, and deploy sophisticated autonomous agents for a diverse range of real-world applications. We understand that the path to mastering Agentic AI can seem daunting, filled with theoretical complexities. Therefore, this guide prioritizes clarity and provides a step-by-step approach, ensuring that whether you are a seasoned software developer, a curious student eager to explore the cutting edge of AI, or a visionary technologist seeking to implement groundbreaking solutions, you will find the knowledge and practical skills you need within these pages.

The increasing demand for intelligent systems capable of operating autonomously is undeniable, spanning industries from robotics and automation to software development and beyond. Building these advanced agents necessitates a specialized skillset and a deep understanding of the core tenets of Agentic AI. This book directly addresses this need, offering a practical and no-nonsense guide to constructing the next generation of autonomous artificial intelligence. We delve into the fundamental architectures that underpin agentic systems, exploring the crucial components of perception, knowledge representation, reasoning, planning, learning, and interaction. Through clear explanations, illustrative examples, and practical guidance, you will learn how to harness these concepts and translate them into functional, intelligent agents.

By the end of this guide, you will not only grasp the theoretical underpinnings of Agentic AI but, more importantly, you will be equipped with the actionable knowledge and practical methodologies to design, develop, and deploy your own autonomous intelligent systems. Get ready to roll up your sleeves and actively participate in building the future – one intelligent agent at a time. This book is your essential companion in mastering the art and science of creating truly autonomous artificial intelligence.

# Part 1

## Foundations of Agentic AI

Before we embark on the practical journey of building Agentic AI, it's crucial to establish a solid understanding of the fundamental concepts that underpin this exciting field. Part 1, "Foundations of Agentic AI," will lay this groundwork by clearly defining what Agentic AI is and how it differs from traditional AI and automation. We will explore the essential characteristics of agency, breaking down its various levels and nuances. Furthermore, we will examine the diverse architectural patterns employed in designing intelligent agents and delve into the core cognitive processes that enable them to perceive, reason, plan, and learn. This foundational knowledge will provide the necessary context and vocabulary for the more practical discussions in the subsequent parts of this book.

# Chapter 1

## What is Agentic AI? Defining Autonomy and Intelligence

In an era increasingly shaped by artificial intelligence, a transformative new field is rapidly gaining prominence: **Agentic Artificial Intelligence**, or simply **Agentic AI**. This paradigm shift moves beyond the task-specific focus of traditional AI, aiming to create intelligent entities capable of independent thought, proactive behavior, and autonomous action in complex and dynamic environments.

### Defining Agentic AI: A Leap Beyond Automation and Traditional AI

To truly grasp the significance of Agentic AI, it's crucial to differentiate it from its predecessors: basic automation and traditional artificial intelligence. Automation, at its core, involves executing pre-programmed sequences for well-defined, repetitive tasks, such as a robotic arm welding parts on an assembly line. Traditional AI, while capable of learning intricate patterns and making complex predictions within specific domains – think of a medical diagnosis system analyzing patient data – typically operates under human-defined goals and often requires ongoing supervision or specific triggers.

Agentic AI, in contrast, strives for a much higher degree of self-direction and initiative. Consider a modern smart factory. While automated robots perform specific assembly tasks, an agentic AI system might oversee the entire production line, autonomously identifying bottlenecks, re-allocating resources, predicting maintenance needs, and even negotiating with suppliers – all with minimal direct human intervention. Similarly, a basic recommendation engine suggests movies based on past viewing history, whereas an agentic personal AI might proactively learn your broader interests, anticipate your needs, and even initiate tasks like booking tickets for an event it knows you'd enjoy.

At its heart, Agentic AI seeks to imbue artificial systems with the fundamental properties of **agents**. In the established framework of computer science and AI, an agent is an entity that perceives its environment through sensors and acts upon that environment through effectors. Agentic AI builds upon this foundation by integrating advanced cognitive capabilities, enabling these agents to reason logically, learn from experience, formulate strategic plans, solve problems creatively, and ultimately, make independent decisions to achieve their defined or inferred objectives. This pursuit of autonomous action distinguishes Agentic AI as a key frontier in the evolution of intelligent systems.

**Exploring the Rich Spectrum of Agency: Levels and Granular Definitions**

The concept of "agency" is the very essence of Agentic AI, a multifaceted attribute that exists not as a binary switch but as a rich and complex spectrum. Understanding the varying levels and granular components of agency is fundamental to both analyzing the capabilities of current Agentic AI systems and to effectively designing the more sophisticated agents of the future.

We can conceptualize agency as a multi-dimensional construct, encompassing several key facets:

- **Reactivity:** At the most basic level, an agent perceives and responds to immediate environmental stimuli. A simple example is an anti-virus program that reacts to the detection of a malicious file by quarantining it.
- **Proactivity:** Agents exhibiting proactivity take initiative and pursue goals without direct external commands. Imagine an AI-powered calendar assistant that proactively schedules meeting times based on participants' availability and even sends out reminders.
- **Goal-Orientedness:** Agentic AI is fundamentally driven by objectives, whether explicitly programmed or inferred from high-level directives. An autonomous robot navigating a warehouse has the overarching goal of delivering goods efficiently.

- **Planning and Problem-Solving:** Higher levels of agency involve the ability to formulate multi-step plans and devise solutions to overcome obstacles in pursuit of goals, especially in complex environments. Consider an AI chess-playing agent that plans several moves ahead to checkmate its opponent.
- **Learning and Adaptation:** Sophisticated agents can learn from their interactions and experiences, continuously refining their performance and adapting their behavior. A self-driving car learns optimal driving routes and adapts to changing traffic conditions based on real-time data.
- **Social Ability (in Multi-Agent Systems):** In scenarios with multiple agents, the ability to interact, communicate, negotiate, and collaborate becomes crucial. Think of a swarm of drones coordinating to perform a complex task like search and rescue.
- **Autonomy:** The overarching principle, representing the agent's capacity for independent operation and decision-making without constant human supervision. This ranges from a partially autonomous system that suggests actions to a fully autonomous system that executes tasks independently for extended periods.

## Granular Components of Agency: A Deeper Dive into Capabilities

Beyond these broad levels, we can further dissect agency by examining specific, more granular capabilities that contribute to an agent's overall autonomy and effectiveness:

- **Perception Range and Fidelity:** This refers to how much of the environment the agent can sense (e.g., a robot's visual field, a software agent's access to data) and the detail and accuracy of that sensory input. A higher perception range and fidelity allow for more informed decision-making.
- **Decision-Making Complexity:** This describes the sophistication of the agent's reasoning processes, ranging from simple rule-based systems to advanced machine learning models capable of probabilistic inference and complex pattern recognition.
- **Action Repertoire:** This encompasses the variety and sophistication of the actions the agent can perform within its environment, from simple movements to complex manipulations or information processing tasks.
- **Adaptability and Resilience:** This refers to the agent's ability to cope with unexpected situations, recover from errors gracefully, and continue to function effectively in the face of uncertainty and change.
- **Temporal Reasoning:** The ability to understand and reason about time, including planning for future events, understanding the duration of actions, and reacting appropriately to time-sensitive situations.

Understanding these varying levels and granular components provides a more precise framework for analyzing and designing Agentic AI systems. As we move into the practical aspects of building these intelligent agents in the subsequent chapters, this foundational knowledge will be essential for making informed design choices and tackling the inherent complexities of autonomous intelligence.

# Chapter 2

## A Taxonomy of Agent Architectures

Having established a foundational understanding of Agentic AI and the multifaceted nature of agency, we now turn our attention to the structural blueprints that underpin these intelligent systems: **agent architectures**. Just as different types of buildings are designed with specific purposes and constraints in mind, so too are agent architectures crafted to enable particular behaviors and functionalities. Understanding this taxonomy is crucial for choosing the right architectural approach when designing and building your own Agentic AI.

Agent architectures provide a framework for organizing the various components of an intelligent agent, including its perception, reasoning, planning, and action mechanisms. Over the years, several distinct architectural paradigms have emerged, each with its own underlying principles and trade-offs. In this chapter, we will explore some of the most influential and commonly encountered agent architectures, including deliberative, reactive, and hybrid approaches.

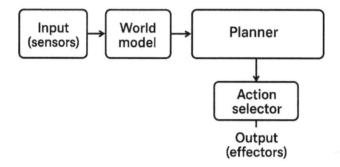

*Figure 2.1:* *This diagram illustrates the fundamental processing steps in a typical deliberative agent architecture. Sensory input is used to build and update an internal world model. A planner then uses this model and the agent's goals to generate a sequence of actions, which are selected and executed via effectors.*

## Deliberative Architectures: The Power of Planning and Symbolic Reasoning

Deliberative architectures, often referred to as cognitive or symbolic architectures, are characterized by their central emphasis on **reasoning and planning** based on an explicit, internal symbolic representation of the world. These agents meticulously construct and maintain a **world model** – a structured repository of their environment, goals, and knowledge, often represented through symbols, rules, and logical relationships. They leverage this model to deliberate on potential actions, formulate detailed plans, and predict the consequences of their choices before committing to execution. A classic example of a domain where deliberative architectures have shown success is in strategic game playing, such as Deep Blue's approach to chess, where extensive lookahead planning is crucial.

Key characteristics of deliberative architectures include:

- **Explicit World Model:** Agents maintain an internal, symbolic representation of their environment. This model might encompass facts ("the door is open"), rules ("if the battery is low, then recharge"), and relationships ("the kitchen is connected to the living room").
- **Goal-Driven Behavior:** Actions are fundamentally driven by explicitly defined goals ("reach the destination," "win the game"). The agent's reasoning and planning processes are geared towards achieving these pre-defined objectives.
- **Planning as a Central Process:** A significant portion of the agent's computational effort is dedicated to planning sequences of actions to achieve its goals. This often involves employing sophisticated search algorithms to explore possible action sequences and evaluate their potential outcomes based on the world model.
- **Complex Reasoning:** Deliberative agents are capable of sophisticated logical reasoning, including deduction (deriving new facts from existing ones), induction (generalizing from

specific instances), and abduction (inferring the most likely explanation).

- **Sequential Processing (Often):** The processes of perceiving the environment, updating the world model, reasoning about goals, formulating plans, and finally executing actions often occur in a sequential or near-sequential manner.

**Strengths of Deliberative Architectures:**

- **Complex Problem Solving:** They excel in tackling intricate problems that necessitate reasoning about abstract concepts, understanding complex relationships, and planning multiple steps into the future.
- **Goal-Oriented Behavior:** The explicit representation of goals makes it relatively straightforward to design agents with clear objectives and to track their progress towards those objectives.
- **Transparency and Explainability (Potentially):** Because their decision-making process is rooted in a symbolic model and explicit reasoning steps, their actions can, in principle, be more transparent and easier for humans to understand and explain.

**Weaknesses of Deliberative Architectures:**

- **Computational Cost:** Maintaining a rich and accurate world model and performing extensive planning, especially in complex or rapidly changing environments, can be computationally very demanding, potentially leading to slow response times.

- **Brittleness in Dynamic Environments:** If the real world changes in ways not anticipated or represented in the agent's world model, the agent's pre-computed plans can become invalid, and the agent may struggle to react effectively in real-time.
- **Difficulty in Handling Uncertainty and Noise:** Symbolic models often struggle to effectively represent and reason with the inherent uncertainty and noisy data present in real-world sensory input.
- **Knowledge Acquisition Bottleneck:** The process of manually building and continuously updating a comprehensive and accurate world model can be a significant knowledge engineering bottleneck, requiring extensive human expertise.

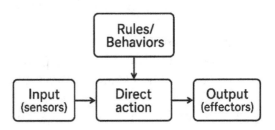

*Figure 2.2: This diagram illustrates the fundamental processing in a reactive agent architecture. Sensory input directly triggers*

*actions based on a set of predefined rules or behavioral modules, bypassing the need for an explicit world model or planning.*

## Reactive Architectures: The Power of Immediate Response and Distributed Control

In stark contrast to the deliberate planning of symbolic systems, reactive architectures prioritize **direct, immediate responses** to sensory input. These agents typically operate without constructing or maintaining a complex, centralized internal world model. Instead, their behavior emerges from a collection of relatively simple, pre-defined stimulus-response rules or direct mappings from perception to action. Subsumption architecture, a prominent example, embodies this philosophy by organizing behaviors in a hierarchy of competence, with lower levels handling basic survival instincts and higher levels managing more complex tasks, all operating in parallel. Reactive robots navigating a cluttered room often rely on such architectures, where immediate sensor readings trigger motor responses to avoid obstacles.

Key characteristics of reactive architectures include:

- **Minimal or No Explicit World Model:** Agents primarily operate based on the current sensory input without relying on a detailed internal representation of their environment's history or future state.
- **Direct Perception-Action Coupling:** Behavior is largely determined by direct, often hard-coded,

mappings from sensory input to specific actions. For instance, "if obstacle detected to the left, turn right."

- **Simple Rules or Behavioral Modules:** The agent's control system is typically composed of a set of relatively simple, independent rules or behavioral modules that can operate concurrently.
- **Parallel Processing:** Multiple sensor-action mappings can often operate in parallel, allowing the agent to respond simultaneously to different stimuli without a central control unit orchestrating every action.
- **Emergent Complexity:** Surprisingly complex and seemingly intelligent behaviors can sometimes emerge from the intricate interactions of numerous simple rules or behavioral modules.

**Strengths of Reactive Architectures:**

- **Fast Reaction Times:** The direct and immediate coupling of perception to action enables very rapid responses to dynamic changes in the environment, crucial for time-sensitive tasks.
- **Robustness in Dynamic and Unpredictable Environments:** They can often adapt effectively to rapidly changing environments because their actions are driven by immediate sensory input rather than potentially outdated internal models.
- **Computational Efficiency:** By avoiding complex modeling and planning, reactive architectures are typically very computationally inexpensive,

making them suitable for resource-constrained systems.
- **Ease of Implementation (Often):** Implementing simple reactive behaviors can often be relatively straightforward.

**Weaknesses of Reactive Architectures:**

- **Lack of Explicit Goal-Directed Behavior (Often):** Achieving complex, long-term goals that require planning and reasoning about the future can be challenging or impossible without a more sophisticated internal representation and planning mechanisms.
- **Difficulty in Complex Problem Solving:** They generally struggle with tasks that necessitate reasoning about the past, future consequences of actions, or aspects of the environment that are not directly perceived.
- **Limited Learning Capabilities (Often):** While some reactive architectures can incorporate learning mechanisms, they often lack the capacity for deep, abstract learning and struggle to generalize to novel situations.
- **Difficult to Design Complex Behaviors Directly:** Designing intricate and coordinated behaviors solely through a large set of stimulus-response rules can become complex, difficult to manage, and hard to predict the overall system behavior.

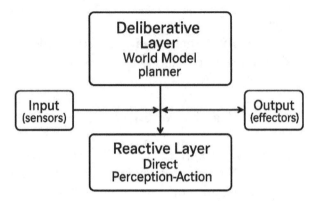

*Figure 2.3:* *This diagram illustrates the fundamental processing in a hybrid agent architecture. Sensory input feeds into both a deliberative layer, responsible for planning based on a world model, and a reactive layer, which directly maps perceptions to actions. The outputs of these layers are then coordinated to produce the agent's behavior.*

**Hybrid Architectures: Blending Deliberation and Reaction for Enhanced Capabilities**

Recognizing the complementary strengths and inherent limitations of purely deliberative and purely reactive architectures, **hybrid architectures** have emerged as a powerful approach to combine elements of both, aiming to create more versatile, robust, and capable agents. These architectures typically integrate multiple distinct layers or interacting components, with higher-level layers often responsible for deliberative functions such as goal setting, planning, and knowledge representation, while lower-level layers handle immediate reactive behaviors for direct interaction with the environment and fast responses to sensory input. Autonomous vehicles, for instance, often employ hybrid architectures where a deliberative layer plans the overall route while reactive layers handle immediate obstacle avoidance and lane keeping.

Key characteristics of hybrid architectures include:

- **Multiple Layers or Interacting Components:** They feature distinct modules or layers designed for different functionalities, such as a planning module and a reactive control module.
- **Integration of Deliberative and Reactive Capabilities:** The core aim is to leverage the strengths of both lookahead planning and fast, immediate responses within a single agent.
- **Coordination Mechanisms:** Sophisticated mechanisms are required to effectively coordinate the activities and information flow between the different layers or components, ensuring coherent overall behavior.
- **Varying Levels of Coupling:** The degree of interaction and influence between the deliberative and reactive components can vary significantly depending on the specific architecture and the application requirements.

**Common Approaches in Hybrid Architectures:**

- **Hierarchical Architectures:** These architectures often feature a hierarchical control structure where higher, deliberative levels set long-term goals and generate abstract plans, which are then refined and executed by lower, reactive levels that directly interact with the environment.
- **Parallel Architectures:** In these designs, deliberative and reactive components may operate concurrently and independently, with mechanisms for arbitration or fusion of their respective outputs to determine the agent's final actions.

**Strengths of Hybrid Architectures:**

- **Balancing Reactivity and Goal-Directedness:** They offer the potential to exhibit both fast, reflexive responses to immediate stimuli and complex, goal-oriented behavior that requires planning and reasoning.
- **Improved Robustness in Dynamic Environments:** The reactive layer can handle immediate, unexpected changes in the environment, while the deliberative layer can adapt long-term plans based on evolving circumstances.
- **Greater Flexibility and Adaptability:** Hybrid architectures can be designed to handle a wider range of tasks and operate effectively in more complex and unpredictable environments compared to purely deliberative or reactive systems.

**Weaknesses of Hybrid Architectures:**

- **Increased Design and Implementation Complexity:** Designing and effectively coordinating the interactions between the different layers or components can be significantly more challenging than designing purely deliberative or reactive systems.
- **Potential for Conflicts and Coordination Issues:** Ensuring seamless and coherent interaction between the deliberative and reactive parts, and resolving potential conflicts between their proposed actions, requires careful and sophisticated design.
- **Design Trade-offs:** Finding the optimal balance between the influence and responsibilities of the deliberative and reactive components often involves significant design trade-offs that can be highly application-dependent.

## Suitability for Various Applications

The selection of an appropriate agent architecture is fundamentally driven by the specific demands of the application.

- **Deliberative architectures** are often best suited for domains that require intricate reasoning, long-term planning, and operation in relatively stable or predictable environments, such as strategic board games, high-level robotic task planning in structured settings, and automated theorem proving.

- **Reactive architectures** excel in dynamic, uncertain, and time-critical environments where rapid responses are paramount, such as autonomous navigation in highly cluttered or rapidly changing spaces, low-level motor control in robotics, and real-time anomaly detection.
- **Hybrid architectures** are frequently the preferred choice for complex, real-world applications that demand a blend of both deliberative planning and reactive execution, such as autonomous vehicles navigating complex traffic scenarios, personal robots interacting with humans in unstructured environments, sophisticated industrial automation systems adapting to changing production demands, and intelligent virtual agents engaging in complex dialogues.

As we progress in this book, understanding these fundamental architectural paradigms will be crucial for making informed decisions about how to structure your own Agentic AI systems to achieve the desired levels of autonomy, intelligence, and capability for your specific applications.

# Chapter 3

## Core Cognitive Processes in Agents

Having explored the fundamental architectures that provide the structural framework for intelligent agents, we now turn our attention to the very engines of their intelligence: the **core cognitive processes**. These processes are the computational mechanisms that enable agents to perceive their environment (like a robot using its cameras to "see"), reason about it (like an AI doctor diagnosing a condition), formulate plans (like a navigation system charting a route), make decisions, and learn from their experiences (like a game-playing AI improving its strategy). A deep understanding of these processes is essential for designing and building Agentic AI that can operate effectively and autonomously in complex and dynamic worlds.

These core cognitive processes are often intricately intertwined, working in concert to enable intelligent behavior. For instance, an autonomous drone might perceive its surroundings using sensors, reason about the best path to avoid obstacles, plan its flight trajectory, and learn from past flights to optimize its energy consumption.

In this chapter, we will undertake an in-depth exploration of several key cognitive processes that are fundamental to the operation of intelligent agents. These include:

- **Perception:** The process by which agents gather information about their environment through sensors and interpret this raw data into a meaningful representation.
- **Reasoning:** The ability of agents to draw inferences, solve problems, and make logical deductions based on their knowledge and perceived information.
- **Planning:** The process through which agents formulate sequences of actions to achieve their goals, considering the current state of the environment and the potential consequences of their actions.
- **Learning:** The capacity of agents to acquire new knowledge, improve their performance, and adapt their behavior over time based on their experiences.

Let's delve into each of these crucial cognitive processes in more detail.

### Perception: Sensing and Interpreting the World

Perception is the agent's crucial gateway to its environment, akin to how humans use their senses to understand the world. It encompasses the acquisition of raw data from various sensors (e.g., cameras, microphones, lidar, tactile sensors for robots; data streams, user inputs, network signals for software agents) and the subsequent processing and interpretation of this data into a usable format. Consider a self-driving car: its perception system uses cameras to "see" lane markings and other vehicles, lidar and radar to measure distances and speeds, and GPS to determine its location. In sophisticated agents, perception often involves:

- **Sensor Fusion:** Combining data from multiple sensors to obtain a more comprehensive and reliable understanding of the environment. For example, that self-driving car might fuse data from its various sensors to create a robust, multi-layered understanding of its surroundings, compensating for the limitations of individual sensors.
- **Feature Extraction:** Identifying relevant features and patterns within the raw sensory data. This could involve an image recognition system detecting edges and shapes to identify objects, a speech recognition system identifying phonemes to understand words, or a financial analysis agent identifying key trends in market data.
- **Pattern Recognition:** Matching extracted features against known patterns to identify objects, events, or situations. This allows an agent to recognize a pedestrian crossing the street, understand a spoken command like "turn left," or detect a fraudulent transaction based on unusual spending patterns.
- **World State Estimation:** Building and maintaining an internal representation (or belief state) of the current state of the environment based on the interpreted sensory information. A robotic vacuum cleaner, for instance, needs to estimate the areas it has already cleaned and the location of obstacles.

The effectiveness of an agent is heavily reliant on the quality and sophistication of its perception capabilities. Noisy or incomplete sensory data, or a flawed interpretation process, can lead to incorrect reasoning, poor planning, and ultimately, ineffective or even dangerous actions.

**Reasoning: Drawing Inferences and Solving Problems**

Reasoning is the cognitive process that allows agents to make sense of the information they perceive and to derive new knowledge or conclusions, much like how a detective uses clues to solve a case. It involves manipulating internal representations of knowledge and applying logical rules or probabilistic models to draw inferences, answer questions, and solve problems. Several forms of reasoning are commonly employed in agentic systems:

- **Logical Reasoning:** This involves applying formal rules of logic (e.g., propositional logic, predicate logic) to deduce new facts from existing ones. For example, if a logistics agent knows "all perishable goods must be refrigerated" and "strawberries are perishable goods," it can logically deduce that "strawberries must be refrigerated."
- **Probabilistic Reasoning:** In situations involving uncertainty, agents often use probabilistic methods (e.g., Bayesian networks, Markov models) to reason about the likelihood of different events or states. A weather forecasting AI, for instance, uses probabilistic reasoning to estimate

the chance of rain based on various atmospheric conditions. This allows agents to make informed decisions even when information is incomplete or noisy.

- **Abductive Reasoning:** This involves inferring the most likely explanation for a set of observations. It's often used in diagnostic tasks or when trying to understand the causes of events. For example, if a system monitoring a server observes high CPU usage and slow response times, it might abductively reason that a specific process is likely consuming excessive resources.
- **Commonsense Reasoning:** This is the ability to make inferences and judgments based on general knowledge about the world that humans typically take for granted. For example, understanding that water flows downhill or that people usually feel happy when they receive a gift. Enabling agents with robust commonsense reasoning remains a significant and ongoing challenge in AI.

The ability to reason effectively is crucial for agents to make informed decisions, solve novel problems that go beyond pre-programmed responses, and operate intelligently in complex and often unpredictable environments.

## Planning: Formulating Action Sequences to Achieve Goals

Planning is the cognitive process by which agents decide on a sequence of actions to achieve their desired goals, much like a human planning a trip or a project. It involves considering the current state of the environment, the agent's capabilities, and the potential consequences of different actions. Effective planning often requires:

- **Goal Formulation:** Clearly defining the objectives that the agent needs to achieve. For an autonomous robot tasked with cleaning a room, the goal might be "the room is free of visible dust and debris." These goals can be explicitly given or derived from higher-level directives.
- **State Space Search:** Exploring the possible sequences of actions and their resulting states to find a path that leads to the goal. An AI navigating a maze might use algorithms like A* search to find the shortest path to the exit.
- **Action Modeling:** Understanding the effects of the agent's actions on the environment. A robotic arm needs a model of how its joints move and how those movements affect the objects it interacts with.
- **Plan Evaluation and Selection:** Assessing the quality of different plans based on factors such as cost (e.g., time, energy), risk, and likelihood of success, and selecting the most appropriate plan to execute.
- **Hierarchical Task Planning (HTN):** Breaking down complex goals into a hierarchy of smaller, more manageable sub-tasks. For example, "clean the room" might be broken down into "vacuum the floor," "dust the surfaces," and "empty the trash."

- **Reinforcement Learning (RL)-Based Planning:** Learning optimal action policies through trial and error by interacting with the environment and receiving rewards or penalties for their actions. This is particularly useful in dynamic and uncertain environments where explicit models are difficult to obtain, such as training a robot to perform complex manipulations.

Robust planning capabilities enable agents to achieve complex goals that require multiple steps, navigate intricate environments effectively, and act strategically over time, anticipating potential challenges and optimizing their actions.

## Learning: Acquiring Knowledge and Improving Performance

Learning is the cognitive process that allows agents to acquire new knowledge, refine their existing skills, and adapt their behavior in response to their experiences, much like how humans learn new skills or improve existing ones through practice. This ability to improve over time is a fundamental characteristic of intelligent systems. Several key learning paradigms are employed in Agentic AI:

- **Supervised Learning:** Learning a mapping from inputs to outputs based on labeled training data. For example, training an AI to classify emails as spam or not spam using a dataset of emails labeled accordingly.

41

- **Unsupervised Learning:** Discovering patterns and structure in unlabeled data. Anomaly detection systems in cybersecurity, for instance, might use unsupervised learning to identify unusual network activity without prior knowledge of specific attack signatures.
- **Reinforcement Learning (RL):** Learning optimal behavior through trial and error by interacting with the environment and receiving rewards or penalties for their actions. Training an AI to play video games or control a robot to perform complex tasks often utilizes reinforcement learning.
- **Imitation Learning:** Learning by observing and mimicking the behavior of an expert. This can be useful for bootstrapping the learning process or for teaching agents complex skills that are difficult to define explicitly, such as training a robot to perform a specific surgical procedure by watching a surgeon.

The ability to learn and adapt is crucial for agents to operate effectively in novel or changing environments where pre-programmed knowledge might be insufficient, to improve their performance on tasks over time, and to achieve increasingly complex and nuanced goals.

As we continue our exploration into building Agentic AI, we will delve deeper into how these core cognitive processes are implemented, integrated, and orchestrated within different agent architectures to create truly intelligent and autonomous systems capable of tackling real-world challenges.

# Part 2

# Designing the Cognitive Architecture

**Designing the Cognitive Architecture** delves into the practical aspects of building the internal "mind" of an intelligent agent. We will explore how to architect robust **perception modules** to enable agents to effectively sense and interpret their environment, even when faced with noisy or ambiguous data. Next, we will examine the design of **memory and belief systems**, crucial for representing and managing an agent's knowledge about the world and itself. We will then move on to the implementation of various **reasoning mechanisms**, allowing agents to draw inferences and solve problems. Finally, we will cover **planning and action selection**, focusing on how agents formulate goals and choose sequences of actions to achieve them, ultimately bridging the gap between thought and action.

# Chapter 4

## Architecting Perception Modules

As we discussed in the previous chapter, perception is the crucial first step in enabling an agent to interact intelligently with its environment. The quality and reliability of an agent's perception system directly impact its ability to reason effectively, plan soundly, and ultimately, achieve its goals. Designing robust perception modules is therefore paramount in the development of effective Agentic AI. This chapter will delve into the fundamental principles that guide the architecture of such systems, along with techniques for handling the inherent challenges of noisy and ambiguous data and for effectively fusing information from multiple sensors.

### Principles of Building Robust Perception Systems

Building a robust perception system for an intelligent agent is a multifaceted endeavor that requires careful consideration of several key principles:

- **Modularity and Abstraction:**

*Figure 4.1: A simplified block diagram illustrating the modular flow of information through a typical perception system, from raw sensor input to the agent's perceived understanding of the world state. Each module performs a specific stage of processing, allowing for a structured and robust approach to perception.*

A well-designed perception module should be modular, meaning it's composed of distinct, interconnected sub-components, each responsible for a specific aspect of the perception process (e.g., raw sensor input, preprocessing, feature extraction, object recognition). Think of a robotic vision system where one module handles image capture, another performs edge detection, and a third identifies objects based on those edges. Abstraction is key to managing complexity, allowing higher-level cognitive processes to interact with the perception module through well-

46

defined interfaces without needing to know the intricate details of its internal workings. This promotes reusability, maintainability, and easier debugging.

- **Handling Sensor Characteristics:** Different sensors have unique characteristics, including their sensing range (e.g., a camera's field of view versus a lidar's range), resolution (the detail they can capture), accuracy (how close their measurements are to the truth), noise profiles (the types and amount of errors they introduce), and data formats (e.g., images, point clouds, time series). A robust perception system must be designed to accommodate these variations. This might involve specific preprocessing steps tailored to each sensor type to calibrate the data (e.g., correcting for lens distortion in a camera), filter out specific types of noise (e.g., removing static from an audio signal), or transform it into a consistent format suitable for downstream processing.
- **Real-Time Processing:** For many agentic applications, particularly those involving physical interaction with the world (like robotics or autonomous vehicles), the perception system must be capable of processing sensory data in real-time or near real-time. For an autonomous car, delays in perceiving an obstacle could have severe consequences. Efficient algorithms (e.g., optimized convolution neural networks for image processing) and hardware acceleration (e.g., using

GPUs or specialized AI chips) may be necessary to achieve the required processing speeds and ensure timely responses.

- **Error Detection and Recovery:** Perception systems are not infallible. Sensors can malfunction (e.g., a camera lens might be obstructed), data transmission can be corrupted (e.g., signal loss in a wireless sensor network), and interpretation algorithms can make mistakes (e.g., misclassifying an object in an image). A robust system should incorporate mechanisms for detecting these errors and, where possible, recovering from them. This might involve cross-checking information from multiple sources (e.g., verifying an object detection with both camera and lidar data), using redundancy in sensor data (e.g., having overlapping fields of view from multiple cameras), or implementing sanity checks on the interpreted information (e.g., flagging an object detection that is physically impossible given the context).

- **Adaptability and Calibration:** The characteristics of sensors can change over time due to environmental factors (e.g., temperature fluctuations affecting sensor readings, wear and tear on mechanical components) or the agent's own movement (e.g., vibrations affecting a robot's sensors). A robust perception system should ideally include mechanisms for self-calibration (e.g., automatically adjusting camera parameters based on observed patterns) and adaptation to these changing conditions (e.g., dynamically adjusting noise filters based on the current environment) to maintain accuracy and reliability over the agent's lifespan.

- **Contextual Awareness:** Perception is not just about processing raw data; it's also about interpreting that data within the broader context of the agent's goals, its current situation, and its prior knowledge. For example, a robot navigating a kitchen might interpret a "red object" differently if it's near the stove (likely a pot) versus on the floor (potentially a dropped toy). A robust system should leverage this contextual information to disambiguate sensory input, filter out irrelevant information, and focus on the most salient aspects of the environment for the agent's current task.

- **Computational Efficiency:** While accuracy and robustness are paramount, the perception system must also be computationally efficient, especially for resource-constrained agents (e.g., small mobile robots) or those operating in real-time with strict latency requirements. There is often a trade-off between the complexity of perception algorithms (which might offer higher accuracy) and their computational cost (which impacts processing speed and energy consumption). Careful design, efficient algorithm selection, and potentially specialized hardware are crucial to finding the right balance for the specific application.

**Handling Noisy and Ambiguous Data**

A significant and constant challenge in architecting perception modules is dealing with the inherent noise and ambiguity present in real-world sensory data.

- **Noise Reduction:** Noise refers to random or systematic errors that corrupt the sensory signals, obscuring the true underlying information. Techniques for noise reduction include various filtering methods (e.g., Kalman filters for tracking dynamic objects with noisy measurements, moving averages to smooth out temporal fluctuations, Gaussian filters to blur high-frequency noise in images) that aim to smooth out the data and remove unwanted fluctuations while preserving the underlying signal. The choice of filtering technique depends critically on the statistical characteristics of the noise and the frequency content of the desired signal.

- **Dealing with Uncertainty:** Uncertainty arises from fundamental limitations in sensor accuracy (e.g., a GPS sensor might have a margin of error), incomplete information (e.g., a camera's view might be partially occluded), or inherent randomness in the environment (e.g., the unpredictable movement of pedestrians). Robust perception systems often employ probabilistic methods (e.g., Bayesian inference to update beliefs based on new evidence, Kalman filters to estimate the state of a system with uncertainty, probabilistic graphical models to represent complex dependencies between variables) to explicitly represent and reason about this uncertainty. Instead of providing a single, definitive interpretation of the data, these methods provide a probability distribution over possible interpretations, allowing higher-level cognitive processes to make more informed decisions and manage risk in the face of ambiguity.

- **Disambiguation Techniques:** Ambiguity occurs when the sensory data can be interpreted in multiple plausible ways. For example, a blurry image might be interpreted as several different types of objects, or a spoken phrase might have multiple possible transcriptions. Contextual information, as mentioned earlier, plays a crucial role in disambiguation. For example, an object detected as "animal" might be further disambiguated as a "cat" if it's observed indoors and moving in a feline manner. Machine learning techniques, particularly sophisticated classification algorithms trained on large and diverse datasets, can also be highly effective in disambiguating ambiguous sensory input by learning to associate specific patterns with the most likely interpretations based on vast amounts of training data.
- **Active Perception:** In some cases, the agent can actively manipulate its sensors or its position in the environment to reduce noise and ambiguity and gather more informative data. For example, a robot might move its camera to get an unobstructed view of a partially occluded object, a

51

sonar system might emit a sweep of different frequencies to better discern the material properties and shape of submerged objects, or a software agent might actively query additional data sources to resolve conflicting information. This active gathering of information can significantly improve the reliability and accuracy of perception.

## Techniques for Sensor Fusion and Information Interpretation

Many advanced Agentic AI systems rely on data from multiple heterogeneous sensors to achieve a more comprehensive, robust, and reliable understanding of their environment than could be achieved by any single sensor in isolation. **Sensor fusion** is the critical process of intelligently combining data from these diverse sources to produce a unified representation that is more accurate, complete, and informative.

- **Data-Level Fusion:**

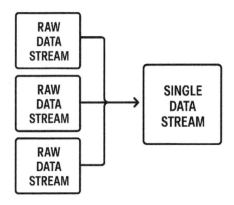

*Figure 4.2:* *Data-level sensor fusion. This diagram illustrates how raw data streams from various sensors (e.g., Camera 1, Lidar, Radar) are directly combined at the data level into a unified data stream for subsequent processing. This technique requires sensor compatibility in terms of data format and sampling rate.*

This involves combining raw sensor data directly before any high-level feature extraction or interpretation. For example, averaging the raw pixel values from multiple cameras observing the same scene to reduce random noise. This approach typically requires the sensors to be relatively compatible in terms of data format, sampling rate, and calibration.

- **Feature-Level Fusion:**

53

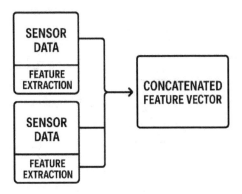

*Figure 4.3:* *Feature-level sensor fusion. This diagram shows how features are extracted independently from the data of different sensors (Sensor A and Sensor B) and then combined (e.g., concatenated) into a unified feature vector. This allows for the integration of complementary information from heterogeneous sensors.*

This involves extracting relevant features from each sensor's data independently and then combining these extracted features into a unified feature vector that captures complementary information from all sensors. For example, combining edge features extracted from a camera image with surface normal features extracted from a lidar point cloud to improve the accuracy and robustness of object recognition. This allows for the fusion of data from heterogeneous sensors that provide different types of information.

- **Decision-Level Fusion:**

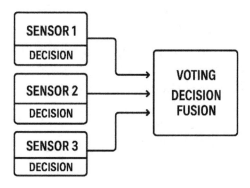

**Figure 4.4**: *Illustration of decision-level sensor fusion. Each sensor independently produces a decision, which is then combined in a central fusion module. In this example, a voting mechanism is used to resolve discrepancies and produce a final consensus decision.*

This involves each sensor making its own independent interpretation or decision about the environment, and then combining these individual decisions using techniques like majority voting, weighted averaging based on sensor reliability, or more sophisticated methods like Bayesian inference or Dempster-Shafer theory to arrive at a final, more reliable and consistent conclusion. This approach is particularly useful when the sensors provide different types of high-level information or have varying levels of reliability for different aspects of the environment.

**Information interpretation** goes beyond simply processing and fusing sensor data; it involves making sense of the integrated information in the context of the agent's goals, its current situation, and its prior knowledge. This often involves:

- **Object Recognition and Categorization:** Identifying and classifying objects in the environment based on their perceived and fused features. This typically involves using sophisticated machine learning models, such as deep convolutional neural networks trained on massive datasets of labeled objects, to recognize a wide variety of entities.
- **Scene Understanding:** Building a coherent and semantically meaningful interpretation of the overall environment, including the spatial layout of objects, their relationships to each other, and the overall context of the scene. This can involve techniques from computer vision, spatial reasoning, knowledge representation, and natural language processing to create a rich understanding of the agent's surroundings.
- **Event Detection and Recognition:** Identifying and understanding significant events occurring in the environment, such as a door opening, a person performing an action, or a specific sound being heard. This often involves temporal reasoning to understand sequences of observations over time and pattern recognition techniques to identify characteristic signatures of different events.

Architecting effective perception modules that adhere to these fundamental principles and intelligently employ appropriate techniques for handling noisy and ambiguous data, as well as for fusing and interpreting information from diverse sensors, is a critical and challenging step towards building truly capable, reliable, and autonomous Agentic AI systems that can effectively operate in the complexities of the real world.

# Chapter 5

## Designing Memory and Belief Systems

Once an agent can perceive its environment, the next crucial step in building a sophisticated cognitive architecture is enabling it to retain and utilize that information over time. This is the role of **memory and belief systems**. These systems allow agents to represent and manage knowledge about their environment, themselves, and the relationships between them. The way an agent stores, retrieves, and updates this information fundamentally shapes its reasoning, planning, and overall behavior. This chapter will explore the key considerations in designing such systems, including different types of memory architectures and the mechanisms by which agents update their beliefs as they interact with the world.

### Representing Knowledge and Beliefs: The Agent's Internal World Model

The way an agent represents knowledge and beliefs is a foundational design choice that influences the efficiency and effectiveness of all subsequent cognitive processes. This internal representation acts as the agent's world model. Several approaches are commonly used:

- **Symbolic Representations:**

## Symbolic Representation

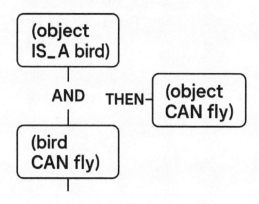

*Figure 5.1:* *Symbolic Representation. This diagram illustrates how knowledge can be represented using symbols and logical rules. The example shows how the rule "IF (object IS_A bird) AND (bird CAN fly) THEN (object CAN fly)" can be used to infer that a given object can fly if it is a bird.*

These involve using symbols, rules, and logical structures to represent explicit facts and relationships. For example, in a rule-based expert system designed to diagnose equipment failures, knowledge might be represented as "IF temperature is high AND pressure is low THEN pump failure." Symbolic representations are powerful for logical reasoning, knowledge-based planning, and providing explanations for decisions, but they can struggle with the inherent uncertainty and continuous nature of real-world environments. Representing nuanced sensory data directly in a symbolic form can also be challenging.

- **Probabilistic Representations:**

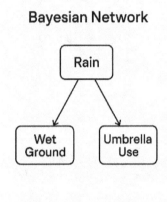

***Figure 5.2:*** *Bayesian Network. This diagram illustrates a simple Bayesian network, a probabilistic graphical model that represents dependencies between variables. In this example, the network shows how "Rain" can influence both "Wet Ground" and "Umbrella Use", demonstrating probabilistic relationships.*

These use probabilities and statistical models (e.g., Bayesian networks to model dependencies between variables, Hidden Markov Models for sequential data) to represent uncertainty and the likelihood of different states or events. This allows agents to reason effectively with incomplete or noisy information, which is common in real-world perception. For example, a self-driving car might represent its belief about the probability of a pedestrian crossing the road based on sensor data and learned patterns.

- **Connectionist Representations:**

*Figure 5.3:* Neural Network. This diagram illustrates a simplified neural network, demonstrating how knowledge is distributed across interconnected nodes. The connections between nodes represent weighted relationships, allowing the network to learn and represent complex patterns.

These involve using artificial neural networks, where knowledge is learned and represented implicitly through the strengths of connections between artificial neurons. Deep learning models excel at pattern recognition in complex sensory data (like images or speech) and learning intricate relationships from large amounts of data. However, the learned representations can be less transparent and harder to interpret or explicitly reason with compared to symbolic approaches.

- **Hybrid Representations:**

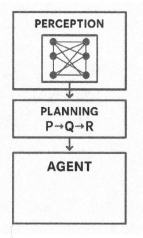

*Figure 5.4: Hybrid Representation. This block diagram illustrates a hybrid approach to knowledge representation within an intelligent agent. Different modules utilize different representation types, such as a neural network for processing sensory input in the perception*

*module, which then feeds into a symbolic planner for decision-making. This allows the agent to leverage the strengths of different representation methods for various tasks.*

Many sophisticated agents, especially those operating in complex real-world scenarios, employ hybrid approaches that strategically combine different representation methods to leverage their respective strengths. For example, a robot might use a neural network for visual perception (connectionist) to identify objects and then use a symbolic planner to decide how to manipulate those objects to achieve a goal (symbolic). The choice of representation often depends on the specific task and the nature of the information being processed.

Beyond the format of representation, the content itself is critical. Agents need to represent:

- **Static Knowledge:** Facts about the world that are generally constant or change very slowly (e.g., "water boils at 100 degrees Celsius at standard pressure," "gravity exists and pulls objects towards the Earth's center"). This forms the foundational understanding of the world.
- **Dynamic Knowledge:** Information about the current state of the environment and how it changes over time (e.g., the current location and velocity of a moving obstacle, the status of a

multi-step task – "step 2 of 5 completed"). This is crucial for real-time decision-making.

- **Episodic Knowledge:** Memories of specific past events and personal experiences, often associated with a specific time, location, and emotional context (e.g., "I encountered a red light at intersection X at 3:15 PM yesterday," "The last time I tried to grasp that object, it slipped"). This allows agents to learn from their history.

- **Procedural Knowledge:** Knowledge about how to perform actions and sequences of actions, often represented as skills or behavioral routines (e.g., "to navigate through a doorway, move forward while ensuring sufficient clearance on both sides," "to answer a common question, retrieve the relevant information from the knowledge base and format it as a natural language response"). This is essential for executing tasks effectively.

- **Self-Knowledge:** Information about the agent itself, including its capabilities (e.g., "can move at a maximum speed of 1 m/s," "has a battery life of 4 hours"), limitations (e.g., "cannot operate in heavy rain," "cannot process more than 10 simultaneous requests"), current state (e.g., "battery level is 75%," "current task is navigation"), and its active goals. This allows the agent to reason about its own actions and capabilities.

- **Beliefs:** These are the agent's current understanding of the world, which may not always be entirely accurate or complete. Beliefs can be based on recent perception, prior knowledge, inferences drawn from available information, or even assumptions made in the absence of complete data. Agents need mechanisms to manage the uncertainty associated with their beliefs.

**Types of Memory Architectures: Storing and Accessing Information**

Different memory architectures have been developed to address the varying needs of intelligent agents in terms of storage capacity, access speed, and the types of information they need to retain and retrieve:

- **Short-Term Memory (STM) / Working Memory:**

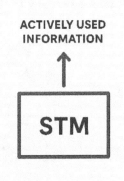

*Figure 5.5: Short-Term Memory (STM). This diagram illustrates the concept of short-term memory (STM) as a small, temporary buffer that*

65

*holds actively used information. STM is crucial for tasks requiring immediate recall and manipulation of information.*

This is a temporary, limited-capacity storage system that holds information currently being actively processed or that is immediately relevant to the agent's ongoing tasks. Think of it as the agent's "scratchpad" for current thoughts and immediate sensory input. Information in STM has a relatively short retention time (seconds to minutes). In cognitive architectures, working memory often serves as a buffer for recently perceived sensory data, the current state of the problem being solved, intermediate results of reasoning processes, and active goals.

- **Long-Term Memory (LTM):**

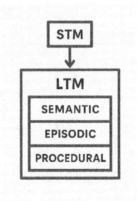

*Figure 5.6:* Long-Term Memory (LTM). This diagram illustrates long-term memory (LTM) as a larger storage system with distinct components for semantic (factual), episodic (event-based), and procedural (skill-based) knowledge. It also depicts the flow of information between short-term memory (STM) and LTM, highlighting the processes of encoding and retrieval.

This is a more permanent storage system with a much larger capacity than STM, designed to store information over extended periods (minutes to years). Accessing LTM can be slower and more effortful than accessing STM, as it involves retrieving information from a larger repository. Different types of LTM are often distinguished:

- **Semantic Memory:** Stores general, factual knowledge about the world, concepts, and relationships between them, independent of specific experiences (e.g., "a bird has feathers," "Paris is the capital of France"). Think of it as an encyclopedia stored in the agent's mind.
- **Episodic Memory:** Stores memories of specific events and personal experiences, often tagged with contextual information such as the time, location, and the agent's emotional state during the event (e.g., "I learned to open a door on Tuesday afternoon in the lab"). This allows the agent to recall specific past situations.

- o **Procedural Memory:** Stores knowledge about how to perform tasks and skills, often acquired through practice and expressed as implicit knowledge of how to execute actions (e.g., how to walk, how to grasp an object). This type of memory is often less accessible to conscious recall but is crucial for efficient action execution.
- **External Memory:**

*Figure 5.7: External Memory Access. This diagram illustrates an intelligent agent accessing an external knowledge source, such as a database or the internet, to retrieve information that supplements its internal memory. This allows the agent to leverage vast amounts of information beyond its direct storage capacity.*

Some agents may also have access to vast amounts of information stored externally, such as databases, knowledge graphs (like Wikidata or ConceptNet), or even the internet. This allows them to access and retrieve information that would be impractical or impossible to store internally. For example, a conversational AI might query a knowledge graph to answer a user's question about a specific topic. The design of how the agent accesses and integrates this external information is a key aspect of its overall memory architecture.

The architecture of the memory system often involves sophisticated mechanisms for transferring information between STM and LTM (e.g., encoding important information from working memory into long-term storage), as well as efficient processes for retrieving relevant information from LTM when needed for reasoning or planning.

## Belief Update Mechanisms: Adapting to a Changing World

As agents actively interact with their environment and continuously receive new sensory information, they need robust mechanisms to update their internal beliefs about the world and themselves to maintain an accurate and consistent understanding. Several mechanisms are used for this:

- **Direct Perception Updates:** The most fundamental way to update beliefs is based on direct sensory input. When an agent perceives a change in its environment (e.g., a robot's vision system detects an obstacle that wasn't there before), it directly updates its belief about the state of the environment to reflect this new information. The reliability of this update is often tied to the perceived trustworthiness of the sensor data.

- **Inference-Based Updates:** Beliefs can also be updated through logical or probabilistic reasoning based on existing beliefs and new evidence. If an agent believes "if the light is red, then I must stop" and it perceives a red light, it can infer and update its belief that it needs to stop. Similarly, probabilistic inference allows for belief updates based on the likelihood of events given new observations.
- **Learning-Based Updates:** Agents can learn from their accumulated experiences and update their beliefs based on patterns they observe or feedback they receive from the environment or other agents. For example, a robot might learn that a certain type of terrain is difficult to traverse based on repeated failures to navigate it successfully, leading to an updated belief about its own mobility capabilities on that terrain.
- **Belief Revision Systems:**

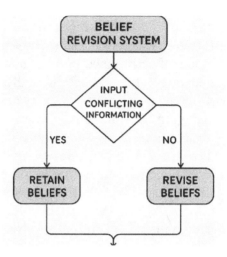

*Figure 5.8:* Simplified Flowchart of a Belief Revision System Handling Conflicting Information.

These are more sophisticated mechanisms designed to handle inconsistencies and conflicts that can arise between new information and an agent's existing set of beliefs. They often involve assigning confidence levels or priorities to different beliefs and employing specific rules or algorithms (like truth maintenance systems or argumentation frameworks) to determine which beliefs to revise or retract when a contradiction is detected. This ensures the agent maintains a coherent and logically consistent internal representation.

- **Probabilistic Updates:** When using probabilistic representations, beliefs are updated using the principles of probabilistic inference, most notably Bayes' theorem. This allows agents to systematically incorporate new evidence by updating the probability distributions over different possible states or events, reflecting the changing likelihoods based on the new observations.

- **Temporal Belief Update:** Agents operating in dynamic environments need to explicitly account for the passage of time and the fact that the world changes even when they are not directly perceiving it. This might involve using models of how the world evolves to predict future states based on current beliefs and then updating those beliefs when new sensory information becomes available. For example, an agent might believe a door is closed but predict that it will open soon if it knows someone is approaching it.

The design of effective belief update mechanisms is absolutely crucial for ensuring that an agent's internal representation of the world remains as accurate and consistent as possible with its ongoing experiences, enabling it to make well-informed decisions and act effectively and adaptively in a constantly changing reality.

# Chapter 6

## Implementing Reasoning Mechanisms

Building upon the agent's ability to perceive and remember information, the next critical step is to equip it with the capacity to **reason**. Reasoning is the cognitive process that allows agents to draw inferences, solve problems, make decisions, and ultimately act intelligently based on their knowledge and beliefs. This chapter will provide a detailed exploration of several key reasoning approaches commonly employed in Agentic AI, including rule-based systems, probabilistic reasoning, and abductive reasoning, along with practical considerations for their implementation.

### Rule-Based Systems: Reasoning with Explicit Rules

Rule-based systems are a fundamental approach to reasoning that relies on a set of explicit **if-then rules** to derive conclusions from a given set of facts. These systems typically consist of three main components:

- **A Knowledge Base:** Contains a set of rules representing knowledge about the domain. Each rule typically has a condition (the "if" part, also known as the antecedent) and an action or conclusion (the "then" part, or consequent). For example, in a medical diagnosis system, a rule might be: "IF patient has fever AND patient has cough THEN patient MAY have influenza."

- **A Working Memory:** Contains the current set of facts or beliefs about the environment and the agent itself. These facts are often derived from perception or prior knowledge. For instance, a robot's working memory might contain facts like "the object is red" and "the object is on the table."
- **An Inference Engine:** A mechanism that applies the rules in the knowledge base to the facts in the working memory to derive new conclusions. The inference engine controls the process of matching rules to facts and triggering the appropriate actions or inferences.

**Implementation Considerations for Rule-Based Systems:**

- **Rule Representation:** Rules can be represented in various formats, from simple "if-then" statements to more complex logical expressions involving conjunctions (AND), disjunctions (OR), and negations (NOT). The choice of representation (e.g., production rules, logical clauses) can significantly impact the expressiveness and efficiency of the system.
- **Inference Engine Algorithms:** Several algorithms can be used for the inference engine:
  - **Forward Chaining (Data-Driven):**

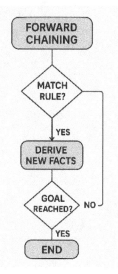

*Figure 6.1:* *Flowchart Illustrating the Forward Chaining Inference Process.*

Starts with the known facts in working memory and applies rules whose conditions are satisfied by these facts to derive new facts, adding them back to the working memory. This process continues iteratively until a specific goal is reached or no new facts can be derived. Forward chaining is well-suited for situations where the initial state is well-defined and the goal is to explore all possible consequences or trigger appropriate actions based on the current situation (e.g., in real-time control systems).

○ **Backward Chaining (Goal-Driven):**

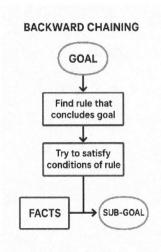

***Figure 6.2:*** *A Simplified Flowchart of Backward Chaining: Reasoning Backwards from a Goal.*

Starts with a specific goal (a hypothesis to be proven or a state to be achieved) and tries to find rules whose conclusion matches the goal. It then works backward, treating the conditions of those rules as new sub-goals that need to be satisfied by the known facts in working memory or by recursively applying the same process to find rules that can prove the sub-goals. Backward chaining is particularly useful for goal-directed reasoning and diagnostic tasks (e.g., in expert systems that try to diagnose a problem).

- ○ **Conflict Resolution:** When multiple rules are applicable (their conditions are met by the facts in working memory) at the same time, a conflict resolution strategy is needed to decide which rule to "fire" (apply). Common strategies include assigning priority levels to rules, selecting the most specific rule (the one with more conditions), or using recency (firing the rule that uses the most recently added facts).
- **Knowledge Acquisition:** Acquiring and encoding the rules in the knowledge base is often a significant bottleneck. It typically requires eliciting knowledge from domain experts and manually translating that knowledge into a set of rules. Automated or semi-automated knowledge acquisition techniques are an active area of research.
- **Scalability and Complexity:** As the number of rules and facts in the system grows, the complexity and computational cost of the inference process can increase dramatically. Efficient indexing of rules, techniques for rule subsumption, and strategies for managing the size of working memory are important for ensuring scalability.
- **Handling Uncertainty:** Basic rule-based systems typically operate on definite facts and produce

definite conclusions. Extending them to handle uncertainty often involves using fuzzy logic (where truth values can range between 0 and 1) or associating probabilities or confidence factors with rules and facts.

## Probabilistic Reasoning: Reasoning Under Uncertainty

Probabilistic reasoning provides a powerful framework for making rational decisions and drawing inferences in situations where information is uncertain, incomplete, or noisy. It involves using the principles of probability theory to represent the likelihood of different states, events, and relationships, and to update these probabilities as new evidence becomes available. Key approaches include:

- **Bayesian Networks (Belief Networks):**

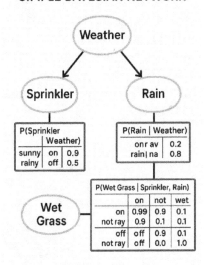

**SIMPLE BAYESIAN NETWORK**

Weather

Sprinkler        Rain

| P(Sprinkler | Weather) | |
|---|---|---|
| sunny | on | 0.9 |
| rainy | off | 0.5 |

| P(Rain | Weather) | |
|---|---|
| onr av | 0.2 |
| rain\| na | 0.8 |

Wet Grass

| P(Wet Grass \| Sprinkler, Rain) | | | |
|---|---|---|---|
| | on | not | wet |
| on | 0.99 | 0.9 | 0.1 |
| not ray | 0.9 | 0.1 | 0.1 |
| off | off | 0.9 | 0.1 |
| not ray | off | 0.0 | 1.0 |

*Figure 6.3:* A Basic Bayesian Network Showing Variables (Nodes) and Their Probabilistic Relationships (Directed Edges), Along with Conditional Probability Tables.

Directed acyclic graphs (DAGs) where each node represents a random variable, and the directed edges represent probabilistic dependencies between these variables. The strength of these dependencies is quantified by conditional probability tables (CPTs) associated with each node, specifying the probability of a variable's states given the states of its parents in the graph. Bayesian inference allows for calculating the

79

posterior probability of some variables (e.g., the probability of rain given that the grass is wet) based on evidence about other variables. Bayesian networks are widely used in areas like medical diagnosis, risk assessment, and fault detection.

- **Markov Models and Hidden Markov Models (HMMs):**

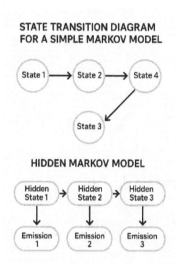

*Figure 6.4: State Transition Diagram for a Markov Model (Top) Showing Observable States, and a Diagram for a Hidden Markov Model (Bottom) Depicting Hidden States and Observable Emissions.*

Markov Models are statistical models that describe a sequence of states, where the probability of transitioning to a future state depends only on the current state (the Markov property). Hidden Markov Models (HMMs) extend this by assuming that the sequence of states is hidden or unobservable, and we only observe a sequence of emissions that are probabilistically dependent on the underlying hidden states. HMMs are particularly useful for modeling sequential data, such as speech recognition, gesture recognition, and time series analysis.

- **Probabilistic Logic Programming:** A field that combines the expressiveness of logic programming (using rules and facts) with the ability to handle uncertainty using probabilities. This allows for building more expressive and flexible reasoning systems that can handle both logical relationships and probabilistic information.

**Implementation Considerations for Probabilistic Reasoning:**

- **Network Structure Design:** For Bayesian networks, designing the graph structure that accurately captures the dependencies between the relevant variables is a crucial and often challenging task, typically requiring significant domain expertise or the use of structure learning algorithms from data.
- **Probability Elicitation:** Obtaining accurate conditional probability tables (CPTs) or

probability distributions can be a significant hurdle, especially for complex domains with many variables. Common methods include eliciting probabilities from domain experts, learning them from large datasets, or using hybrid approaches.

- **Inference Algorithms:** Performing exact inference (calculating precise probabilities) in complex Bayesian networks can be computationally intractable (NP-hard). Therefore, various approximate inference algorithms (e.g., belief propagation, Markov Chain Monte Carlo methods, variational inference) are often employed to provide probabilistic estimates within a reasonable time.
- **Computational Cost:** Probabilistic inference, especially with complex models and large datasets, can be computationally very expensive. Efficient data structures, optimized algorithms, and sometimes specialized hardware are essential for real-time or large-scale applications.
- **Handling Continuous Variables:** Many real-world domains involve continuous variables (e.g., temperature, pressure). Extending basic probabilistic models to handle these often involves using specific probability distributions (e.g., Gaussian distributions) and adapting inference algorithms accordingly.
- **Learning Probabilistic Models:** Agents can learn the structure and parameters of probabilistic models (like Bayesian networks or HMMs) from data using various machine learning techniques,

such as maximum likelihood estimation or Bayesian learning.

## Abductive Reasoning: Reasoning to the Best Explanation

Abductive reasoning is the process of inferring the most likely or best explanation for a given set of observations or evidence. It moves from an observation to a plausible explanation for that observation. For example, if a robot observes a spill on the floor, it might abductively reason that someone likely dropped a drink. Abductive reasoning is crucial for tasks like diagnosis, planning under incomplete information, and natural language understanding.

## Implementation Considerations for Abductive Reasoning:

- **Generating Explanations:** A key challenge is generating a set of plausible explanations that could account for the observed evidence. This often involves using background knowledge, causal models (representing cause-and-effect relationships), and potentially generating hypotheses.
- **Evaluating Explanations:** Once a set of potential explanations has been generated, they need to be evaluated and ranked based on several criteria to determine the "best" explanation:

- o **Plausibility:** How likely is the explanation to be true based on prior knowledge and beliefs?
- o **Consistency:** Does the explanation contradict any known facts or highly probable beliefs?
- o **Completeness (Explanatory Power):** How well does the explanation account for all the observed evidence? A better explanation accounts for more of the observations.
- o **Simplicity (Parsimony):** Following Occam's Razor, simpler explanations that make fewer assumptions are generally preferred over more complex ones.
- **Search Strategies:** Finding the best explanation often involves searching through a potentially large space of possible explanations. Efficient search algorithms (e.g., heuristic search, constraint satisfaction techniques) are needed, especially for complex domains.
- **Handling Uncertainty:** Abductive reasoning often deals with uncertain observations and potential explanations that have varying degrees of likelihood. Integrating probabilistic approaches can provide a way to quantify the uncertainty associated with different explanations.
- **Knowledge Representation for Explanations:** The way background knowledge, causal relationships, and potential explanations are represented (e.g., using semantic networks, causal graphs, logical rules with associated probabilities)

significantly impacts the efficiency of generating and evaluating explanations.

## Integrating Different Reasoning Mechanisms

In many sophisticated Agentic AI systems designed to tackle complex real-world problems, relying on a single reasoning mechanism is often insufficient. Hybrid cognitive architectures that strategically integrate different reasoning techniques are becoming increasingly prevalent. For example, an agent might use rule-based reasoning for well-defined, procedural tasks, probabilistic reasoning for handling the inherent uncertainty in sensory perception and prediction, and abductive reasoning for diagnosing unexpected situations or generating creative solutions when faced with novel problems. The design of how these different reasoning modules interact, share information, and coordinate their outputs is a critical aspect of building advanced and adaptable Agentic AI.

As we continue our exploration into the design of Agentic AI, a thorough understanding of the strengths and weaknesses of these different reasoning approaches, along with the practical considerations for their effective implementation and integration, will be essential for building truly intelligent agents capable of robust and adaptive behavior in complex real-world challenges.

# Chapter 7

## Planning and Action Selection

Having equipped our agent with the ability to perceive, remember, and reason, we now turn to the crucial cognitive processes of **planning and action selection**. These processes enable an agent to exhibit goal-oriented behavior by deciding what actions to take and in what sequence to achieve its objectives. Effective planning involves anticipating the consequences of actions, considering available resources and constraints, and formulating a course of action that is likely to lead to the desired outcome. Action selection, on the other hand, involves choosing the specific action to execute at each step, often based on the current plan and the immediate state of the environment. This chapter will explore various techniques for achieving goal-oriented behavior, delve into specific planning methodologies like Hierarchical Task Networks (HTNs) and Reinforcement Learning-based planning, discuss other action selection mechanisms, and finally, examine the critical aspect of integrating planning with execution.

### Techniques for Goal-Oriented Behavior: Charting a Path to Success

Achieving goal-oriented behavior in intelligent agents requires more than just having goals; it necessitates sophisticated mechanisms to translate those goals into coherent and effective sequences of actions. Several key techniques underpin this crucial capability:

- **Goal Representation:** The very first step is to clearly and unambiguously represent the agent's goals. This can range from simple, well-defined state-based goals (e.g., a robot needing to "reach location X" with specific coordinates) to more complex objectives involving multiple conditions, temporal constraints, or preferences (e.g., an autonomous delivery agent needing to "deliver package Y to customer Z by 5:00 PM while minimizing travel time and avoiding traffic"). The choice of goal representation (e.g., using logical predicates, temporal logic, or utility functions) significantly influences how easily the agent can reason about and plan to achieve them.

- **State-Space Search:**Many classical planning algorithms operate by systematically searching through the space of possible states that the agent can be in as a result of its actions. Starting from an initial state (the agent's current situation), the agent explores potential sequences of actions and their resulting successor states, aiming to find a path (a sequence of actions) that leads to a desired goal state. Fundamental algorithms like Breadth-First Search (BFS), Depth-First Search (DFS), and informed search algorithms like A* search are commonly employed for this purpose. Heuristics (problem-specific knowledge used to estimate the distance to the goal from a given state) play a crucial role in guiding the search process and making state-space search efficient, especially in complex domains with a large number of possible states.

- **Plan Evaluation and Optimization:** Once one or more potential plans (sequences of actions) have been generated, they need to be evaluated based on various criteria to determine their quality and feasibility. These criteria can include the plan's cost (e.g., total execution time, energy consumption, resource utilization), its length (number of steps), the inherent risk associated with the actions in the plan, and the overall likelihood of success in achieving the goal. Agents often need to optimize their plans to find the most efficient, safest, or otherwise desirable way to achieve their objectives. Techniques like dynamic programming, genetic algorithms, and various other optimization algorithms can be employed for this purpose.

- **Constraint Satisfaction:** Many real-world planning problems are subject to various constraints that must be satisfied during plan execution (e.g., a robot's limited battery life, strict deadlines for task completion, physical limitations on movement or manipulation). Constraint satisfaction techniques can be integrated directly into the planning algorithms or applied as a post-processing step to ensure that the generated plans are feasible and adhere to all relevant constraints. Constraint Programming (CP) is a powerful paradigm for modeling and solving such problems.

- **Goal Decomposition:** For complex, high-level goals, a common and effective strategy is to break them down into a hierarchy of simpler, more manageable sub-goals. This "divide and conquer" approach can significantly reduce the complexity of the planning process. Hierarchical Task Networks (HTNs), which we will discuss in more detail below, are a prime example of a planning paradigm that heavily relies on goal decomposition.

**Hierarchical Task Networks (HTNs): Planning with Domain Knowledge**

Hierarchical Task Networks (HTNs) are a sophisticated planning paradigm that leverages domain-specific knowledge about how tasks can be decomposed and achieved. Unlike classical planning which primarily searches through state space, HTN planning primarily searches through a space of task decompositions.

- **Task Decomposition:** The core idea of HTN planning is to represent tasks and sub-tasks in a hierarchical structure, forming a network. For example, the high-level task "prepare a meal" might be decomposed into sub-tasks like "prepare ingredients," "cook main course," and "set the table." Each of these sub-tasks can be further decomposed until primitive actions are reached.
- **Methods:** HTN planning uses "methods" to specify how a non-primitive task can be decomposed into a partially ordered or totally

ordered sequence of sub-tasks. A single non-primitive task might have multiple applicable methods, and the choice of method often depends on the current state of the world and the agent's capabilities.

- **Primitive Actions:** These are the basic, executable actions that the agent can directly perform in its environment (e.g., "move to location," "grasp object," "turn on switch"). These actions form the leaves of the task network.
- **HTN Planner:** An HTN planner takes an initial state and a top-level task as input and searches for a sequence of primitive actions (a plan) by recursively applying task decomposition methods until all tasks in the network are primitive. The output is a plan (a sequence of primitive actions) that, when executed, should achieve the initial goal. HTN planning is particularly effective in domains where significant procedural knowledge is available.

**Reinforcement Learning for Planning: Learning by Trial and Error**

Reinforcement Learning (RL) offers a fundamentally different approach to planning, especially well-suited for dynamic, uncertain, and complex environments where creating explicit models of the environment and the effects of actions is challenging or impossible. In RL-based planning, an agent learns an optimal policy (a strategy for selecting actions in each state) through trial and error by interacting with the environment and receiving scalar rewards or penalties for its actions.

- **Markov Decision Processes (MDPs):** [*Consider a visual aid here: A diagram illustrating the interaction loop in Reinforcement Learning, showing the agent in a state, taking an action, transitioning to a new state, and receiving a reward.*] RL problems are often formalized as Markov Decision Processes (MDPs), which are defined by a set of states, a set of possible actions in each state, transition probabilities (the probability of moving from one state to another after taking a specific action), and a reward function (which specifies the immediate reward or penalty received after a transition).
- **Policies:** A policy $\pi$ defines the agent's behavior; it is a mapping from states to actions, specifying which action the agent should take in each state. The goal of RL is to learn an optimal policy $\pi*$ that maximizes the agent's cumulative reward over time (the expected sum of discounted future rewards).
- **Value Functions:** Many RL algorithms involve learning value functions, which estimate the "goodness" of being in a particular state (state-value function) or taking a particular action in a particular state (action-value function) in terms of expected future rewards.
- **Exploration vs. Exploitation:** A fundamental challenge in RL is the trade-off between exploration (trying out new actions to discover

potentially better strategies and learn more about the environment) and exploitation (using the currently known best policy to maximize immediate reward). Effective RL algorithms need to balance these two aspects.

- **Deep Reinforcement Learning:** Recent breakthroughs in deep learning have led to the development of deep reinforcement learning algorithms, where deep neural networks are used to approximate value functions or policies. This has enabled RL to be applied to complex, high-dimensional state and action spaces, such as learning to play complex video games from raw pixel inputs or controlling sophisticated robots.

**Other Action Selection Mechanisms: Beyond Planning**

While planning aims to generate a sequence of actions to achieve a goal, action selection mechanisms often operate at a more immediate level, deciding which action to take at the current time step based on the agent's internal state and the perceived environment.

- **Behavior-Based Systems:** As discussed in Chapter 2, these systems are composed of a collection of independent, task-achieving behavioral modules that directly map sensory input to specific actions. Action selection in these systems typically involves arbitration mechanisms (e.g., winner-take-all, weighted blending) that determine which behavior should be active and thus which action should be executed at any given moment based on the current sensory input and the agent's priorities or internal state.

- **Utility-Based Systems:** These systems assign a utility value (a measure of desirability or "goodness") to different states of the world or to taking specific actions in a given state. The agent then selects the action that is expected to lead to the state with the highest utility or the action with the highest expected utility. This approach allows for decision-making under uncertainty and the consideration of multiple potentially conflicting goals.
- **Subsumption Architecture:** A specific and influential type of behavior-based architecture where behaviors are organized in a hierarchical structure of competence. Lower-level behaviors (e.g., obstacle avoidance) that are crucial for survival or immediate response can directly suppress the actions proposed by higher-level, more goal-directed behaviors (e.g., navigating to a target location) if necessary. This architecture emphasizes robustness and reactivity.

**Integrating Planning with Execution: Bridging the Gap Between Thought and Action**

Generating a plan is only the first step towards achieving a goal; the agent must also be able to reliably execute that plan in a dynamic and often unpredictable real world. This integration of planning and execution presents several key challenges:

- **Plan Monitoring:** During execution, the agent needs to continuously monitor the actual outcomes of its actions and compare them with the predictions made during the planning phase. This allows for the detection of deviations, unexpected events, or outright failures in plan execution.
- **Error Detection and Recovery:** When discrepancies between the planned and actual outcomes are detected, or when unexpected events occur, the agent needs mechanisms to identify these situations and attempt to recover. This might involve trying alternative actions within the current plan, adjusting the remaining steps of the plan, or even abandoning the current plan and engaging in replanning.
- **Replanning:** In highly dynamic or unpredictable environments, the initial plan might become entirely invalid or suboptimal due to unforeseen circumstances. The agent may need to replan from its current state to achieve its original goal or a revised goal. The speed and efficiency of the replanning process are crucial for the agent's responsiveness and ability to adapt.
- **Execution Monitoring and Control:** The agent needs to have mechanisms to precisely control the execution of its chosen actions, ensuring that they are performed correctly and in the intended sequence. This often involves feedback loops between the perception system (providing information about the effects of the actions) and the action execution mechanisms (e.g., motor control in a robot).

- **Deliberation Scheduling:** In hybrid cognitive architectures that combine deliberative planning with reactive behaviors, there needs to be a principled mechanism for deciding when to engage in computationally intensive planning and when to rely on faster, more reactive responses. This scheduling can be based on factors like the complexity of the current situation, the time constraints for action, the agent's confidence in its current plan, or the perceived stability of the environment.

The seamless and robust integration of planning and action selection is a fundamental requirement for creating truly autonomous agents that can effectively pursue and achieve their goals in the complexities of the real world.

# Part 3

## Implementing Key Agent Capabilities

**Implementing Key Agent Capabilities** shifts our focus to the practical construction of intelligent agents. We will explore the development of **Goal Management Systems**, detailing how agents define, prioritize, and break down their objectives. Next, we'll delve into **Building Interaction and Communication Modules**, covering how agents engage with their environment, other agents, and humans through various protocols, including natural language. We will then examine **Implementing Learning and Adaptation**, focusing on practical approaches to integrate different learning paradigms for continuous improvement. Finally, we will discuss **Modular Code Design Patterns for Agents**, providing reusable blueprints and code examples for building common agent components.

# Chapter 8

## Developing Goal Management Systems

The ability to pursue and achieve goals is a defining characteristic of intelligent agents. However, for agents to operate effectively in complex environments and handle multiple objectives, they require sophisticated **Goal Management Systems**. These systems are responsible for defining the agent's goals, prioritizing them when conflicts arise, managing their progress, and adapting them as the environment changes or new information becomes available. Furthermore, Goal Management Systems often incorporate mechanisms for **goal decomposition** (breaking down high-level goals into smaller, more manageable sub-goals) and **task planning** (developing sequences of actions to achieve these sub-goals and ultimately the main objectives). This chapter will explore the key aspects of designing such systems.

**Designing Systems for Defining, Prioritizing, and Managing Agent Goals: The Engine of Agency**

A robust Goal Management System needs to address several critical functions, acting as the very engine that drives the agent's behavior:

- **Goal Definition and Representation:** The first step is to have a clear, expressive, and flexible way to define and represent the agent's goals. Goals can originate from various sources, including explicit user commands (e.g., "make a restaurant reservation"), internal drives or motivations (e.g., a robot needing to recharge its battery when its power is low), or environmental cues (e.g., detecting a fire triggering a "extinguish fire" goal). They can range from simple, one-time objectives (e.g., "send a confirmation email") to complex, long-term aspirations (e.g., an AI tutor aiming to improve a student's understanding of a subject over several weeks). The representation of goals can vary significantly depending on the agent's architecture and the complexity of its tasks. Common representations include:

- State-Based Goals: Defining a desired state of the world that the agent aims to achieve. For example, in a navigation task, the goal might be represented as "the robot's location = (X, Y)."
- Action-Based Goals: Specifying an action or a sequence of actions that the agent needs to perform. For instance, a smart home agent might have a goal to "turn on the living room lights at 7:00 PM."
- Utility-Based Goals: Defining goals in terms of maximizing a utility function that reflects the agent's preferences and the desirability of different states or outcomes. For example, a trading agent might have a goal to maximize profit, with different

trading actions having associated expected utilities.

- o **Temporal Goals:** Goals that have associated time constraints, such as deadlines or specific time windows for achievement. An example is a delivery drone with the goal to "deliver the package to address A by 10:00 AM."

- **Goal Prioritization and Conflict Resolution:** Agents often find themselves with multiple active goals, some of which may be in conflict due to limited resources or environmental constraints, or they may have varying levels of importance to the agent or its users. A sophisticated Goal Management System must include robust mechanisms for prioritizing these goals and resolving conflicts when they arise. Common prioritization strategies include:

  - o **Static Priorities:** Assigning fixed levels of importance to different goal types based on the agent's design or user specifications. For example, a safety-critical goal like "avoid collision" might always have the highest priority for an autonomous vehicle.

  - o **Dynamic Priorities:** Adjusting goal priorities based on the current situation, urgency, or progress towards other goals. For instance, a "find charging station" goal for a robot might increase in priority as its battery level decreases.

  - o **Utility-Based Prioritization:** Prioritizing goals based on their current and expected future contribution to the agent's overall utility or reward. Goals with a higher potential payoff might be given precedence.

- o **Preemption:** Allowing higher-priority goals to temporarily interrupt or suspend the pursuit of lower-priority goals. For example, a "respond to emergency" goal might preempt a lower-priority "clean the floor" goal for a service robot.

- **Goal Management and Monitoring:** Once goals are defined and prioritized, the system needs to actively manage their lifecycle and monitor the agent's progress towards them. This involves:
  - o **Goal Tracking:** Maintaining a record of the agent's current set of goals, their status (e.g., active, pending execution, in progress, completed, failed, suspended), and any associated deadlines, constraints, or dependencies on other goals.
  - o **Progress Monitoring:** Continuously assessing the agent's progress towards achieving its active goals, often by monitoring relevant environmental variables (e.g., distance to a target location) or internal states (e.g., percentage of task completed). This allows the agent to know how well its actions are leading to the desired outcomes.
  - o **Goal Achievement Detection:** Determining when a goal has been successfully achieved based on predefined

criteria (e.g., a target state is reached, a specific action has been performed, a utility threshold has been met).

- o **Goal Failure Detection:** Identifying situations where a goal is no longer achievable due to environmental changes, resource depletion, or repeated failures, or where the cost of continuing to pursue the goal outweighs the potential benefits.

- **Goal Revision and Adaptation:** The environment in which an agent operates is rarely static, and the agent's own capabilities and understanding can evolve over time. Therefore, a crucial aspect of a robust Goal Management System is its ability to revise and adapt goals. This includes:

  - o **Goal Modification:** Adjusting existing goals based on new information, changing environmental conditions, or feedback received during goal pursuit. For example, if a delivery route is blocked, the navigation goal might need to be modified to find an alternative path.

  - o **Goal Abandonment:** Deciding to stop pursuing a goal if it becomes irrelevant (e.g., a requested item is no longer available), unachievable (e.g., a critical resource is depleted), or no longer desirable (e.g., a higher-priority goal makes it obsolete). The decision to abandon a goal often involves a cost-benefit analysis.

- Goal Adoption: Accepting new goals that arise dynamically from the environment (e.g., responding to a sudden obstacle), user input (e.g., a new request), or internal reasoning (e.g., inferring a new need based on the current situation). The agent needs mechanisms to evaluate and integrate these new goals into its existing set of objectives.

## Goal Decomposition and Task Planning: From Abstract Intentions to Concrete Execution

Many high-level goals that an intelligent agent needs to achieve are too abstract or complex to be accomplished through a single, simple action. **Goal decomposition** is the essential process of breaking down these abstract goals into a hierarchical structure of smaller, more concrete sub-goals. **Task planning** then involves developing detailed sequences of actions (plans) to achieve these sub-goals, and by extension, the original high-level goal.

- **Goal Decomposition Techniques:**
  - **Hierarchical Task Networks (HTNs):** As discussed in Chapter 7, HTNs provide a powerful and structured way to decompose tasks based on domain-specific knowledge about how complex activities are typically performed.
  - **Problem Reduction:** Breaking down a complex problem into a set of smaller,

ideally independent sub-problems whose individual solutions can be combined to form a solution to the original problem. This is common in problem-solving domains like theorem proving or puzzle solving.

- o **Means-Ends Analysis:** A problem-solving strategy that involves identifying the difference between the current state and the desired goal state, and then selecting actions (means) that are expected to reduce this difference. This process can recursively lead to the creation of new sub-goals to address the identified differences.
- **Task Planning Approaches:** Once goals and sub-goals have been defined and decomposed, a task planner is needed to generate a detailed sequence of actions to achieve them. Various planning approaches can be employed, each with its own strengths and weaknesses:
  - o **Classical Planning:** Using formal representations of states, actions (with preconditions and effects), and goals to find a sequence of actions that provably leads from a well-defined initial state to a goal state. Languages like STRIPS and the Planning Domain Definition Language (PDDL) are commonly used to model such planning problems.
  - o **Heuristic Search Planning:** Employing heuristic functions to estimate the "distance" to the goal in a large state space,

guiding search algorithms like A* to find efficient plans. These heuristics are often domain-specific and crucial for scalability.

- o **Planning under Uncertainty:** Developing plans that can account for uncertain action outcomes or incomplete information about the environment. Techniques include probabilistic planning, contingent planning (which specifies different action sequences depending on possible outcomes), and conformant planning (which aims to find a plan that works regardless of the initial uncertainty).
- o **Reinforcement Learning for Planning:** Learning policies that directly map states to actions to achieve long-term goals through interaction with the environment and the receipt of rewards. This approach excels in domains where explicit models are unavailable or difficult to create.
- **Integration of Goal Decomposition and Task Planning:** Goal decomposition and task planning are often tightly intertwined. The hierarchical structure of goals and sub-goals provided by decomposition can significantly guide and constrain the search space for the task planner. For example, an HTN planner directly uses decomposition methods to generate a plan as a sequence of primitive actions. In other architectures, the decomposed sub-goals might serve as intermediate objectives that a classical or heuristic planner then tries to achieve.

Designing an effective and adaptive Goal Management System that can seamlessly define, prioritize, manage, decompose, and plan for goals is absolutely crucial for enabling intelligent agents to exhibit complex, autonomous, and flexible behavior in a wide range of challenging real-world applications.

# Chapter 9

## Building Interaction and Communication Modules

For an intelligent agent to effectively operate in the world, collaborate with other agents, and seamlessly assist humans, it must possess robust **Interaction and Communication Modules**. These modules are responsible for enabling the agent to perceive and act upon its environment, exchange information and coordinate with other artificial entities, and engage in meaningful and intuitive dialogue with human users. This chapter will delve into the key aspects of building such modules, focusing on the intricacies of communication protocols for inter-agent communication, the multifaceted challenges of natural language interaction for human-agent communication, and the growing importance of multimodal interaction.

### Enabling Interaction with the Environment: The Agent's Embodiment and Action

An agent's ability to interact with its environment is not merely a feature; it is the very foundation of its agency and its capacity to perceive, learn, and ultimately achieve its goals. This interaction typically involves two tightly coupled and essential aspects:

- **Action Execution:** The agent needs to possess the means to physically or virtually manipulate its environment, translating its internal decisions and plans into tangible changes in the external world. This crucial capability requires **actuators** or **effectors** that can execute the agent's commands. For a physical robot operating in the real world, these might include a diverse range of components such as motors for locomotion and joint movement, grippers and manipulators for object interaction, and speakers for auditory output. For a software agent operating in a digital environment, these might involve making API calls to external services, modifying data structures within a system, or displaying information and receiving input through a graphical user interface. The design of the action execution module must carefully consider the agent's specific physical or virtual embodiment, its repertoire of capabilities, the precision and reliability of its effectors, and the inherent constraints and dynamics of the environment in which it operates. For example, a robotic arm needs precise motor control to grasp a delicate object without crushing it, while a software agent sending an email needs to adhere to network protocols and email formatting standards.
- **Environmental Feedback:** Critically, after executing an action, the agent needs to be able to perceive and interpret the consequences of that action through its sensory inputs. This feedback loop is absolutely crucial for verifying the success

of the action (did it have the intended effect?), detecting any unexpected or unintended outcomes (did something else change in the environment?), and updating the agent's internal model of the environment to reflect the new state. The continuous interaction between action and perception forms a fundamental closed-loop control system that is essential for robust, adaptive, and goal-directed behavior. Without accurate and timely feedback, an agent would be operating blindly, unable to correct errors or adjust its future actions based on the actual results of its past behavior. For instance, a self-driving car needs constant feedback from its cameras and lidar to adjust its steering and speed based on the road conditions and the movement of other vehicles.

## Enabling Interaction and Communication with Other Agents: The Foundation of Multi-Agent Systems

In multi-agent systems (MAS), where multiple autonomous agents interact to achieve individual or collective goals, the ability for agents to effectively interact and communicate with each other is absolutely vital for coordination, collaboration, negotiation, and achieving common objectives that might be beyond the capabilities of a single agent. This necessitates the careful design and implementation of appropriate communication protocols and shared understandings:

- **Communication Protocols:** These are well-defined sets of rules, conventions, and message formats that govern how agents exchange information. They dictate the structure, content, and intended meaning of messages, as well as the permissible sequences of interactions between agents. Different types of communication protocols exist, each carefully tailored to address specific needs and interaction scenarios:
  - **Low-Level Protocols:** These protocols deal with the fundamental physical or network layer of communication, ensuring the reliable and ordered transmission of raw data bits between agents. Examples include TCP/IP for network communication, Bluetooth for short-range wireless interaction, and shared memory mechanisms for agents operating on the same computational platform.
  - **Mid-Level Protocols:** These protocols define the structure, syntax, and basic semantics of the messages exchanged between agents. Agent Communication Languages (ACLs), such as the FIPA ACL standards, provide frameworks that specify common "speech acts" or communicative intents, like "inform" (conveying information), "request" (asking another agent to perform an action), "promise" (committing to a future action), and "query-if" (asking about the truth of a proposition). These protocols

aim to provide a degree of standardization and facilitate interoperability between different agent systems.

- ○ **High-Level Protocols:** These protocols build upon the mid-level protocols to define more complex interaction patterns and conventions for specific types of collaborative activities, such as negotiation (for resource allocation or conflict resolution), task allocation (for distributing work among agents), and information sharing (for collective knowledge building). Examples include the Contract Net Protocol for task bidding and various multi-agent negotiation protocols.

- **Message Content and Semantics:** For communication to be effective, the content of messages exchanged between agents needs to be meaningful, unambiguous, and easily interpretable by the receiving agent. This often requires the development and adoption of shared ontologies – formal and explicit specifications of conceptualizations, including the definitions of terms, their properties, and the relationships between them. Shared ontologies provide a common vocabulary and semantic framework that enables agents to understand the meaning behind the messages they exchange, even if they were developed by different teams or use different internal knowledge representations.

- **Communication Architectures:** The underlying architecture that supports inter-agent communication can significantly impact the efficiency, scalability, and robustness of the multi-agent system. Different architectures include:
    - **Direct Communication:** Agents communicate directly with each other, establishing point-to-point connections. This can be efficient for small, tightly coupled groups of agents but can become complex as the number of agents increases.
    - **Mediated Communication:** Agents communicate indirectly through a central facilitator, message broker, or blackboard system. This can simplify communication management and enable more flexible interaction patterns but introduces a potential single point of failure.
    - **Blackboard Systems:** Agents share information by posting and reading messages, data, or partial solutions on a common, shared data structure (the "blackboard"). This allows for asynchronous and opportunistic collaboration.
- **Coordination and Collaboration:** Effective communication is the bedrock upon which agents can coordinate their individual actions and collaborate on complex tasks that require the combined efforts and diverse capabilities of multiple agents. This often involves sophisticated

communication protocols for negotiation (reaching mutually acceptable agreements), planning joint actions (developing shared plans to achieve common goals), and resolving conflicts (addressing disagreements or competing resource demands).

## Enabling Interaction and Communication with Humans: Bridging the Natural Language Gap

For many intelligent agents, particularly those designed to directly assist or interact with human users in a natural and intuitive way (such as virtual assistants, chatbots, and service robots), the ability to communicate in natural language is a paramount requirement. **Natural Language Interaction (NLI)** aims to bridge the gap between human linguistic expression and the structured, symbolic processing of artificial intelligence. Building robust NLI capabilities involves tackling several intricate and interconnected challenges:

- **Natural Language Understanding (NLU):** This is the crucial process of enabling an agent to process and interpret human language input, transforming raw text or speech into a structured, machine-understandable representation of the user's meaning and intent. It encompasses a series of complex sub-tasks:
  - **Lexical Analysis:** Identifying individual words and their basic morphological forms (e.g., stemming, lemmatization).

- **Syntactic Parsing:** Analyzing the grammatical structure of sentences to understand the relationships between words and phrases (e.g., identifying subjects, verbs, objects).
- **Semantic Interpretation:** Determining the meaning of individual words and phrases within the specific context of the utterance and the broader discourse. This often involves mapping linguistic expressions to formal semantic representations.
- **Discourse Analysis:** Understanding the relationships between consecutive sentences and the overall coherence and meaning of a conversation or text. This includes tasks like co-reference resolution (identifying which entities are being referred to across multiple sentences).
- **Intent Recognition:** Identifying the user's underlying goal or the specific action they want the agent to perform based on their linguistic input (e.g., "book a flight," "play some music," "set an alarm").
- **Entity Extraction:** Identifying and categorizing key entities (e.g., names of people, dates, locations, products) mentioned in the user's input that are relevant to their intent.

- **Natural Language Generation (NLG):** This is the complementary process of enabling an agent to produce fluent, coherent, and contextually appropriate human-like language output to respond to the user, provide requested information, or proactively ask clarifying questions. It involves a sequence of steps:

- o **Content Planning:** Deciding what information needs to be conveyed to the user based on the agent's internal knowledge and the context of the interaction.
- o **Sentence Planning:** Structuring the sentences to be generated, including choosing appropriate grammatical structures and organizing the information logically.
- o **Surface Realization:** Generating the actual words and phrases, ensuring grammatical correctness, appropriate vocabulary, and a natural and engaging style.

- **Dialogue Management:** This critical component is responsible for managing the overall flow and coherence of a conversation between the agent and the human user. It involves:
  - o **Turn-Taking:** Deciding when the agent should listen for user input and when it should produce its own output.
  - o **Context Tracking:** Maintaining a representation of the ongoing dialogue, including the topics discussed, the entities mentioned, and the user's goals and preferences, to correctly interpret new

utterances in context and generate relevant responses.

- ○ **Response Generation:** Selecting appropriate and informative responses based on the user's current input, the tracked context, and the agent's overall goals.
- ○ **Error Handling:** Gracefully dealing with misunderstandings, ambiguous or ungrammatical input from the user, and situations where the agent cannot fulfill the user's request. This often involves asking clarifying questions or offering alternative solutions.

- **Multimodal Interaction:** Increasingly, human-agent interaction is evolving beyond the sole use of language to incorporate multiple sensory modalities, such as vision (e.g., interpreting hand gestures, facial expressions), audio (e.g., recognizing tone of voice, prosody), and haptics (e.g., providing tactile feedback). Building agents that can seamlessly understand and generate information across these diverse modalities adds a significant layer of complexity but also promises richer, more natural, and more intuitive interaction experiences. For example, a social robot might understand a user's frustration not just from their words but also from their facial expression and tone of voice, and might respond with both verbal reassurance and a comforting gesture.

Building effective Interaction and Communication Modules that enable agents to seamlessly engage with their environment, collaborate effectively with other agents, and communicate naturally and intuitively with humans is a critical and ongoing endeavor in the field of Agentic AI. The multifaceted challenges involved in natural language interaction, and the emerging complexities of multimodal interaction, underscore the significant effort required to truly bridge the gap between artificial and natural intelligence and create AI systems that can be genuine partners and assistants to humans.

# Chapter 10

## Implementing Learning and Adaptation

A cornerstone of intelligent agency is the capacity to learn from experience and adapt behavior over time, leading to continuous improvement, enhanced robustness, and the ability to tackle novel situations effectively. This chapter will delve into practical strategies for integrating the three fundamental machine learning paradigms – supervised learning, unsupervised learning, and reinforcement learning – into the core architecture of intelligent agents. We will explore how each paradigm contributes to specific agent capabilities, discuss architectural considerations for their synergistic integration, and briefly touch upon the inherent trade-offs and challenges.

**Harnessing Supervised Learning for Enhanced Agent Capabilities: Learning from Labeled Wisdom**

Supervised learning, where an agent learns a function that maps inputs to outputs based on a rich dataset of labeled examples, provides a powerful mechanism for endowing agents with sophisticated perceptual and predictive abilities:

- **Advanced Perception:** Supervised deep learning models, such as Convolutional Neural Networks (CNNs) for image processing and Recurrent

Neural Networks (RNNs) for sequence data [1] (like audio or video), have revolutionized agent perception. Trained on large, labeled datasets, agents can achieve high accuracy in tasks like object recognition (identifying and classifying objects in their environment), scene understanding (interpreting the spatial relationships and semantic context of a visual scene), and robust speech recognition (transcribing spoken language into text).

- **Predictive Modeling and Forecasting:** Agents can learn to predict future states of the environment, the likely outcomes of their own or others' actions, or even user behavior by training on historical sequences of states, actions, and their observed consequences. This predictive capability is paramount for effective planning (anticipating the results of different action sequences), decision-making under uncertainty (estimating the probabilities of different outcomes), and risk assessment (forecasting potential hazards). For instance, a logistics agent might learn to predict delivery times based on traffic patterns and weather conditions.
- **Classification and Categorization for Reasoning:** Supervised learning enables agents to categorize complex situations, classify objects into predefined categories, or identify the type of event occurring based on learned patterns in sensor data or textual input. A medical diagnosis agent might classify a patient's condition based on their symptoms, or a spam detection agent could

categorize emails as spam or not spam based on their content and metadata.

- **Behavioral Cloning: Imitating Expertise:** Agents can learn to mimic the behavior of human or artificial experts by observing and learning from labeled demonstrations, where expert states are paired with the corresponding actions they took. This "learning by imitation" or "behavior cloning" can be particularly valuable for bootstrapping complex tasks where explicitly defining a reward function for reinforcement learning is challenging, such as learning complex motor skills for robotics or emulating expert driving behavior in autonomous vehicles.

## Practical Integration Strategies:

- **Modular and Encapsulated Learning Components:** Designing agent architectures with well-defined, modular learning components dedicated to specific supervised tasks. These modules should have clear interfaces for receiving input data and providing learned outputs (e.g., a trained object recognition module providing object labels to the reasoning module).
- **Robust Data Pipelines and Annotation Frameworks:** Establishing efficient and scalable data collection, annotation, and management pipelines is crucial for providing the high-quality labeled data required for effective supervised learning. This includes developing user-friendly

annotation tools and strategies for ensuring data consistency and accuracy.

- **Systematic Model Selection and Evaluation:** Implementing rigorous frameworks for selecting appropriate supervised learning models based on the task requirements and data characteristics, and for evaluating their performance using relevant metrics (e.g., accuracy, precision, recall, F1-score, AUC for classification; mean squared error, R-squared for regression). Cross-validation and hyperparameter tuning are essential steps in this process.
- **Continuous Learning and Adaptive Model Updates:** Designing mechanisms that allow agents to continuously update their supervised models with new labeled data encountered during operation. This enables adaptation to evolving environments, changing user preferences, or the discovery of new patterns. Techniques like online learning and fine-tuning pretrained models are relevant here.

**Unveiling Hidden Structures with Unsupervised Learning: Discovering Knowledge in the Unknown**

Unsupervised learning, where agents learn to find inherent patterns, structures, and relationships within unlabeled data, provides crucial capabilities for environmental understanding, knowledge discovery, and anomaly detection:

- **Automated Feature Extraction and Representation Learning:** Unsupervised techniques like autoencoders, dimensionality reduction methods (e.g., PCA, t-SNE, UMAP), and clustering algorithms can enable agents to automatically discover salient features and develop more efficient and robust representations of their sensory inputs or internal states without relying on explicit labels. This can significantly simplify subsequent learning and reasoning processes by focusing on the most informative aspects of the data.
- **Clustering and Categorization of Novelty:** Unsupervised learning algorithms allow agents to group similar data points into clusters, effectively identifying natural categories within their experience. Furthermore, by learning the characteristics of these clusters, agents can detect anomalies or unusual patterns that deviate significantly from the learned normal behavior, which is critical for tasks like fault detection in machinery or identifying unusual user activity.
- **Generative Modeling for Imagination, Planning, and Data Augmentation:** Generative models learned through unsupervised learning (e.g., Variational Autoencoders (VAEs), Generative Adversarial Networks (GANs)) can enable agents to imagine potential future states, simulate the consequences of actions, or even generate synthetic data to augment their training sets for other learning tasks. This can be particularly valuable for planning in complex

121

environments or for improving the robustness of supervised learning models.

**Practical Integration Strategies:**

- **Unsupervised Preprocessing for Feature Engineering:** Integrating unsupervised learning techniques as initial preprocessing layers in a larger agent architecture to automatically extract meaningful features from raw data before feeding it into supervised or reinforcement learning modules, potentially reducing the need for manual feature engineering.
- **Exploratory Data Analysis and Knowledge Discovery Tools:** Utilizing unsupervised learning methods to analyze the agent's operational data, uncover hidden patterns, identify correlations, and potentially discover new knowledge or insights that might not be apparent through labeled data analysis alone.
- **Initialization and Regularization through Unsupervised Pretraining:** Leveraging unsupervised pretraining on large amounts of unlabeled data to initialize the weights of deep neural networks, providing a better starting point for subsequent supervised learning and often leading to improved performance and faster convergence. Unsupervised learning principles can also inspire regularization techniques that encourage the learning of more generalizable and robust representations.

- **Continuous Monitoring for Novelty and Change Detection:** Incorporating unsupervised learning models to continuously monitor the agent's sensory inputs and internal states for the emergence of novel patterns, significant changes in data distributions, or the detection of anomalies that might require adaptive responses, trigger further investigation, or indicate a need for retraining.

## Empowering Agents with Reinforcement Learning for Adaptive and Goal-Oriented Behavior

Reinforcement learning (RL), where agents learn optimal behaviors by interacting with an environment and receiving scalar rewards or penalties for their actions, is particularly powerful for enabling agents to learn complex sequences of actions to achieve goals and adapt their behavior in dynamic and uncertain environments:

- **Learning Optimal Policies for Complex Tasks:** RL algorithms enable agents to learn policies (mappings from states to actions) that maximize their cumulative reward over time in intricate and dynamic environments. This is applicable to a wide range of challenging tasks, including robotic control, autonomous navigation, strategic game playing, and resource management in complex systems.
- **Autonomous Adaptation to Dynamic Environments:** RL agents can continuously adapt their behavior in response to changes in the

environment, the behavior of other agents, or their own internal state by learning from the ongoing stream of rewards and penalties. This adaptability is crucial for agents operating in real-world scenarios where conditions can change unpredictably.

- **Learning from Sparse or Delayed Rewards for Long-Term Goals:** RL can handle tasks where the reward signal is sparse or delayed, requiring the agent to learn long sequences of actions that eventually lead to a positive outcome, even if the immediate consequences of individual actions are not directly rewarding. This is essential for solving complex problems that require strategic planning over extended time horizons.

**Practical Integration Strategies:**

- **Careful Design of Reward Functions:** Meticulously crafting reward functions that accurately incentivize the desired agent behavior and align with its overall goals is paramount for successful RL. Poorly designed reward functions can lead to unintended or suboptimal behaviors.
- **Effective State and Action Space Engineering:** Defining appropriate state representations that capture all the relevant information from the environment while remaining manageable for the learning algorithm, and designing action spaces that allow the agent to effectively interact with the environment are critical steps.

- **Strategic Algorithm Selection and Hyperparameter Tuning:** Choosing suitable RL algorithms (e.g., Q-learning, Deep Q-Networks, Policy Gradient methods like PPO or A2C) based on the characteristics of the task and environment (e.g., discrete vs. continuous action spaces, episodic vs. continuous tasks), and carefully tuning their hyperparameters for stable and efficient learning.
- **Efficient Simulation-to-Reality Transfer Techniques:** Often involving training RL agents in high-fidelity simulated environments to reduce the cost and risk associated with real-world experimentation, followed by the application of techniques like domain randomization or adversarial training to improve the transferability of learned policies to the complexities of the real world.
- **Experience Replay and Sophisticated Exploration Strategies:** Implementing mechanisms for storing and replaying past experiences to improve learning efficiency and stability by allowing the agent to learn from past successes and failures multiple times. Designing effective exploration strategies (e.g., epsilon-greedy, Boltzmann exploration, curiosity-driven exploration) is crucial for encouraging the agent to discover optimal behaviors and avoid getting stuck in local optima.
- **Leveraging Curriculum Learning and Transfer Learning in RL:** Employing curriculum learning (training on a sequence of

progressively more difficult tasks) and transfer learning (leveraging knowledge learned in related tasks to accelerate and improve learning in a new task) to make the learning process more efficient and robust, especially for complex problems.

## Architectural Frameworks for Synergistic Integrated Learning Agents

The effective and synergistic integration of these diverse learning paradigms often necessitates thoughtful architectural design that allows for seamless information flow and coordination:

- **Hybrid Learning Architectures with Information Sharing:** Designing agents with distinct modules dedicated to supervised, unsupervised, and reinforcement learning, but with well-defined interfaces and mechanisms for these modules to share learned representations, knowledge, and insights. For example, features learned through unsupervised learning might be used to improve the performance of a supervised perception module, or the value function learned in RL could be used to guide exploration in a supervised learning task.
- **Memory Systems as Central Knowledge Repositories:** Incorporating sophisticated memory systems that can store and retrieve diverse types of experiences relevant to different learning tasks. For instance, episodic memory can provide valuable data for reinforcement learning

by allowing the agent to replay successful or unsuccessful sequences of actions, while semantic memory can inform supervised learning tasks by providing contextual knowledge. Experience replay buffers are a common example in deep RL.

- **Meta-Learning Frameworks for Learning to Learn:** Exploring meta-learning approaches where the agent learns how to learn more efficiently and adapt more rapidly to new tasks or environments by leveraging experience gained from previous learning episodes. This involves learning generalizable learning strategies or representations that can be quickly adapted to novel situations.

- **Continual Learning Strategies for Lifelong Adaptation:** Implementing techniques that allow agents to continuously learn new information and tasks from a non-stationary data distribution without suffering from catastrophic forgetting of previously learned knowledge. This is a critical challenge for building truly autonomous and adaptive agents that can operate effectively over extended periods in the real world.

**Trade-offs and Challenges in Integrated Learning:**

While the integration of multiple learning paradigms offers significant potential, it also presents several trade-offs and challenges that must be carefully considered:

- **Increased Complexity:** Designing, implementing, and debugging agents with multiple interacting learning modules can be significantly more complex than using a single paradigm.

- **Data Requirements:** Different learning paradigms have different data requirements. Integrating them might necessitate the collection and management of diverse types of data (labeled, unlabeled, interaction data).

- **Computational Costs:** Training and running agents with multiple learning components can be computationally expensive, requiring significant hardware resources and efficient algorithms.

- **Coordination and Interference:** Ensuring that the different learning modules learn synergistically without interfering with each other or leading to instability can be a significant challenge.

- **Defining Clear Objectives and Evaluation Metrics:** When integrating multiple learning goals, defining clear overall objectives and appropriate evaluation metrics to assess the agent's integrated performance can be complex.

Despite these challenges, the potential benefits of creating intelligent agents that can leverage the strengths of different learning paradigms for continuous improvement and adaptation are immense, paving the way for more robust, flexible, and truly intelligent AI systems.

# Chapter 11

## Modular Code Design Patterns for Agents

Building sophisticated and scalable intelligent agents demands the application of sound software engineering principles, with modularity and the strategic use of design patterns being paramount. This chapter will explore a range of reusable architectural blueprints that can serve as high-level guides for structuring an agent system, as well as specific code design patterns that can be effectively applied to the development of common and crucial agent components such as belief states, planners, action selectors, perception modules, and communication interfaces. Our aim is to provide practical guidance, complemented by illustrative code examples (using a Python-like pseudocode for clarity), to empower developers to construct these fundamental building blocks in a structured, maintainable, and extensible manner.

### Architectural Blueprints for Structuring Agent Systems: Guiding the Overall Design

The overall architecture of an intelligent agent provides the foundational structure upon which its various capabilities are built. Several established architectural blueprints offer valuable guidance for organizing the flow of information and control within an agent:

- **Sense-Think-Act (STA) Architecture:** This is a foundational and intuitively understandable blueprint that describes the continuous interaction of an agent with its environment. The agent first **senses** its surroundings through its sensors, then **thinks** about the perceived information, processes it using its internal reasoning, planning, and decision-making modules, and finally **acts** upon the environment using its effectors. This cycle repeats continuously, enabling the agent to react to changes and pursue its goals dynamically. The "Think" component is a crucial abstraction that can encompass a variety of internal modules responsible for belief management, reasoning, planning, and action selection. This architecture is well-suited for simpler agents or as a high-level conceptual model for more complex systems.
- **Model-Based Reflexive Architecture:** This architecture extends the purely reactive approach by incorporating an explicit internal **world model**, which is a representation of the agent's knowledge about its environment, including objects, their properties, and their relationships. The agent **senses** the environment, uses this sensory input to update its internal **world model**, and then selects actions based on reasoning and planning performed on this model. The **action selection** module then triggers the **actuators**. The feedback loop from the environment, through the sensors, to the world model is critical for the agent to maintain an accurate understanding of its surroundings and adapt its actions accordingly.

This architecture enables more sophisticated decision-making in dynamic and partially observable environments.

- **Layered Architectures:** For complex agents that need to handle a wide range of tasks and exhibit different levels of sophistication in their behavior, **layered architectures** provide a powerful way to manage complexity. These architectures organize different control and processing functionalities into a hierarchy of layers, each with specific responsibilities. A common example includes a three-layer architecture: a **reactive layer** for immediate responses to sensory input, a **deliberative layer** for long-term planning and reasoning, and an **executive layer** for coordinating the activities of the other layers and managing the overall behavior of the agent. This modularity allows for independent development and testing of different aspects of the agent's intelligence and facilitates the integration of different reasoning and learning techniques. Layered architectures are particularly useful for autonomous robots operating in complex real-world environments.

- **Blackboard Architecture:** This architecture centers around a shared data structure called the **blackboard**. Different, independent **knowledge sources** (which can be modules responsible for perception, reasoning, planning, action selection, communication, etc.) can access and contribute to the information on the blackboard. Knowledge sources monitor the blackboard for specific types of data or conditions that trigger their execution. When triggered, a knowledge source processes relevant information from the blackboard and may post new information, update existing information, or trigger actions. This architecture facilitates flexible and opportunistic collaboration between different agent components, especially in systems where the problem-solving process is complex and the sequence of necessary actions is not always predictable. Blackboard architectures are often used in systems like speech recognition and complex planning systems.

**Code Design Patterns for Common Agent Components: Implementing Reusable Building Blocks**

Within these overarching architectural blueprints, specific code design patterns provide proven solutions to recurring design problems when building individual agent components:

- **Belief State Management:**
  - **Repository Pattern:** As illustrated earlier, this pattern provides a centralized way to manage the agent's beliefs, abstracting away the underlying data storage and retrieval mechanisms. This promotes consistency and simplifies access to the agent's knowledge base from different parts of the system.
  - **Observer Pattern:** Also shown previously, this pattern enables decoupled

communication between components. When the belief state changes, interested observers (e.g., planners that need to react to new information) are automatically notified without the belief management component needing to know the specifics of these observers.

o **Composite Pattern:** For representing hierarchical belief structures or knowledge. For example, an agent's belief about an object might have sub-beliefs about its properties (color, size, location). The Composite pattern allows treating individual beliefs and compositions of beliefs uniformly.

Python

```python
from abc import ABC, abstractmethod

class BeliefComponent(ABC):
    @abstractmethod
    def get_value(self):
        pass

class AtomicBelief(BeliefComponent):
    def __init__(self, value):
        self._value = value
    def get_value(self):
        return self._value

class CompositeBelief(BeliefComponent):
    def __init__(self, key):
        self._key = key
        self._children = []
```

```
    def add(self, child):
        self._children.append(child)
    def get_value(self):
        return              {child._key:
child.get_value()      for     child    in
self._children}
```

- **Planners:**
  - **Strategy Pattern:** As demonstrated before, this pattern allows for the dynamic selection and use of different planning algorithms based on the current context, problem type, or agent capabilities.
  - **Builder Pattern:** Useful for constructing complex planning problems or plans with numerous parameters in a step-by-step, controlled manner, separating the construction of a plan from its representation.
  - **Command Pattern:** Can be used to encapsulate actions within a plan as objects, allowing for queuing, logging, and potentially undoing actions.

Python

```
from abc import ABC, abstractmethod

class Action(ABC):
    @abstractmethod
    def execute(self):
        pass

class MoveForwardAction(Action):
    def __init__(self, distance):
```

```
            self._distance = distance
        def execute(self):
            print(f"Moving      forward      by
{self._distance}")

class Plan:
    def __init__(self):
        self._actions = []
    def add_action(self, action):
        self._actions.append(action)
    def execute(self):
        for action in self._actions:
            action.execute()
```

- **Action Selectors:**
  - o **Strategy Pattern:** As shown previously, this enables the agent to employ different action selection policies (e.g., rule-based, utility-based, learned policies from reinforcement learning) depending on the situation or the agent's current goals.
  - o **Chain of Responsibility Pattern:** Allows for a sequence of action selection rules or filters to be applied. Each handler in the chain decides either to select an action or to pass the decision to the next handler in the chain. This can be useful for implementing prioritized action selection based on different criteria.
- **Perception Modules:**
  - o **Adapter Pattern:** Crucial for integrating diverse sensors or perception subsystems with varying interfaces into a unified internal representation that the rest of the agent can easily consume. This pattern

allows the agent to work with a consistent data format regardless of the underlying sensor technology.

- o **Factory Pattern:** Provides a way to create instances of specific sensor drivers or perception algorithms dynamically based on configuration files or runtime conditions, promoting flexibility and decoupling the agent's core logic from the specific perception components being used.

- **Communication Modules:**
  - o **Strategy Pattern:** Enables the agent to support multiple communication protocols (e.g., different Agent Communication Languages for inter-agent communication, various API formats for interacting with external services) and switch between them as needed based on the communication partner or context.
  - o **Mediator Pattern:** Can simplify complex communication and coordination between multiple agent components by introducing a central mediator object that manages their interactions, reducing direct dependencies between them and promoting looser coupling.

**Benefits of Embracing Modular Code Design:**

Adopting modular code design patterns yields substantial advantages in the development of intelligent agents:

- **Enhanced Reusability:** Components designed using well-established patterns are inherently more reusable across different agent projects or within various parts of a complex agent, reducing development time and effort.
- **Improved Maintainability:** Modular code is significantly easier to understand, debug, test, and modify. Changes within one well-defined module are less likely to have unintended side effects on other parts of the system, simplifying maintenance and updates.
- **Increased Scalability:** The modular nature of patterned designs facilitates the independent development and testing of individual components, making it easier to scale complex agent systems by adding or modifying modules without affecting the entire architecture.
- **Greater Flexibility and Adaptability:** Patterns like Strategy enable the agent to dynamically switch between different algorithms or behaviors at runtime, making the agent more flexible and adaptable to changing environments or task requirements.
- **Enhanced Testability:** Individual modules with well-defined interfaces can be tested in isolation, leading to more thorough and reliable testing, and ultimately, more robust and dependable agents.
- **Improved Collaboration:** Modular designs with clear interfaces facilitate collaboration among different developers or teams working on different parts of the agent system.

By thoughtfully leveraging these architectural blueprints and code design patterns, developers can construct more sophisticated, maintainable, scalable, flexible, and testable intelligent agents, ultimately accelerating the development process and significantly improving the quality and reliability of the resulting AI systems.

# Part 4

## Ensuring Reliability, Safety, and Explainability

**Ensuring Reliability, Safety, and Explainability** addresses the critical challenges of building trustworthy and responsible Agentic AI systems. We will explore **Verification and Validation**, focusing on rigorous testing methodologies for autonomous systems, including simulation, unit, system-level testing, and formal verification. Next, we will delve into **Designing for Robustness and Fault Tolerance**, examining principles and techniques for building resilient agents capable of handling noisy data, unexpected situations, and failures. We will then provide a comprehensive overview of **Explainable Agency**, covering various methods to make agent decisions transparent. Finally, we will discuss **Human-in-the-Loop Control and Oversight**, focusing on strategies for human monitoring, intervention, and the ethical considerations of increasing autonomy.

# Chapter 12

## Verification and Validation of Agentic Systems

As intelligent agents transition from research labs to real-world deployments, often in safety-critical domains such as autonomous transportation, healthcare, and industrial automation, ensuring their reliability, safety, and trustworthiness becomes paramount. **Verification and Validation (V&V)** are indispensable processes for building confidence in these increasingly autonomous systems. Verification aims to rigorously confirm that the agent is built correctly according to its intended specifications ("Are we building the system right?"), focusing on the internal design and implementation. Conversely, validation aims to confirm that the system effectively meets the user's needs, operates safely and as intended in its target environment, and ultimately solves the right problem ("Are we building the right system?"). This chapter will delve into rigorous testing methodologies specifically tailored to the unique challenges of autonomous systems, including the crucial role of simulation environments, the importance of unit and system-level testing, and provide an introduction to the fundamental concepts of formal verification, alongside a glimpse into emerging trends in the field.

## Rigorous Testing Methodologies for Autonomous Systems: Addressing Unique Challenges

Testing autonomous systems presents a distinct set of challenges that go beyond traditional software testing paradigms. The inherent complexity of their behavior, their continuous interaction with dynamic and often unpredictable environments, and their autonomous decision-making capabilities necessitate specialized and rigorous testing methodologies:

- **Comprehensive Scenario-Based Testing:** Autonomous agents are designed to operate in a vast and potentially infinite range of scenarios. Therefore, testing must involve the meticulous definition and execution of a comprehensive suite of test scenarios that cover not only nominal operating conditions but also a wide spectrum of edge cases, including unusual, unexpected, and potentially hazardous situations. These scenarios should be carefully derived from system requirements, thorough safety analyses (e.g., hazard identification and risk assessment), real-world operational data (if available), and even creatively constructed adversarial scenarios designed to probe the limits of the agent's capabilities and robustness. For example, testing an autonomous vehicle would involve scenarios with varying weather conditions, traffic densities, pedestrian behavior, and unexpected road obstacles.

- **Advanced Coverage Metrics for Autonomous Behavior:** Traditional code coverage metrics, which focus on the lines of code executed, are often insufficient for evaluating the thoroughness of testing in autonomous systems. New, more sophisticated metrics are needed that focus on the coverage of the agent's state space (the range of possible internal states the agent can be in), its decision-making logic (the different pathways through its control algorithms), and its interaction patterns with the environment (the variety of sensory inputs and action sequences explored). This might include metrics that quantify the coverage of different goal states achieved, the diversity of explored action sequences, and the range of handled environmental conditions and unexpected events.
- **Quantitative Metrics for Performance and Safety:** Beyond ensuring functional correctness (i.e., the agent performs the intended tasks), rigorous testing must also quantitatively evaluate the agent's performance (e.g., efficiency in task completion, speed of response, accuracy of predictions) and, critically, its safety (e.g., probability of collision, adherence to safety regulations, robustness to sensor noise). This requires defining clear and measurable quantitative metrics that can be automatically collected and analyzed during testing across a wide range of scenarios. For instance, in an autonomous robot, performance might be measured by the time taken to navigate a maze,

while safety could be quantified by the minimum distance maintained from obstacles.

- **Robust Handling of Non-Determinism and Emergent Behavior:** Autonomous agents, particularly those that incorporate learning algorithms like reinforcement learning or operate in complex multi-agent systems, can exhibit non-deterministic behavior (where the same input can lead to different outputs across different runs) or even emergent properties (complex, unintended behaviors arising from the interaction of simpler components). Testing methodologies must account for this inherent variability. This often involves running tests multiple times with different initial conditions and random seeds, and employing statistical analysis to assess the overall robustness, stability, and predictability of the agent's behavior over a large number of trials.

- **The Critical Challenge of Defining Oracles:** Defining clear, reliable, and unambiguous test oracles (mechanisms for automatically or semi-automatically determining the expected outcome of a test) can be particularly challenging for complex autonomous systems. Unlike traditional software where expected outputs for given inputs are often well-defined, the "correct" behavior of an autonomous agent in a complex, dynamic environment can be nuanced and context-dependent. Developing effective oracles might involve using simplified but validated models of the environment or the agent's expected high-level behavior, relying on human expert judgment for complex scenarios, or employing statistical analysis of the agent's behavior over many simulations to identify statistically significant deviations from expected performance or safety metrics.

## The Indispensable Role of Simulation Environments in Testing

Simulation environments have become an absolutely crucial tool in the verification and validation of autonomous systems, offering a multitude of key advantages that are often impossible or impractical to achieve through real-world testing alone:

- **Uncompromising Safety:** Testing in simulation allows for the safe exploration of potentially dangerous and high-risk scenarios (e.g., system failures, extreme environmental conditions, near-miss situations) without any risk of damage to the agent itself, the surrounding environment, or, most importantly, human safety. This enables thorough investigation of failure modes and the evaluation of safety mechanisms in a controlled setting. For example, testing the emergency braking system of an autonomous vehicle in a simulation of a sudden obstacle.
- **Precise Controllability and Reproducibility:** Simulation environments provide a high degree of control over all relevant environmental conditions (e.g., lighting, weather, traffic flow) and the ability to precisely reproduce specific test scenarios as

many times as needed. This is absolutely essential for effective debugging (identifying the root causes of failures), regression testing (ensuring that bug fixes or new features haven't introduced new issues), and systematically evaluating the agent's behavior under identical conditions.

- **Enhanced Scalability and Comprehensive Coverage:** Simulations can be used to efficiently test a vast range of scenarios and explore the agent's behavior in conditions that might be extremely rare, geographically dispersed, or prohibitively expensive or time-consuming to encounter in the real world. This allows for a much more comprehensive coverage of the agent's operational envelope. For instance, simulating thousands of hours of driving in diverse weather conditions for an autonomous vehicle.

- **Rich Instrumentation and Detailed Data Collection:** Simulation environments often provide rich instrumentation capabilities, allowing for the detailed and fine-grained monitoring of the agent's internal states (e.g., memory contents, decision variables), its sensor data (e.g., raw camera images, lidar point clouds), and its actions (e.g., motor commands, communication messages). This facilitates in-depth analysis of the agent's behavior, identification of bottlenecks, and the collection of quantitative data for performance and safety evaluation.

- **Accelerated Development and Iteration Cycles:** Testing in simulation can significantly speed up the overall development and iteration cycle by allowing for rapid experimentation, immediate feedback on design changes, and automated testing pipelines. This enables developers to quickly identify and address issues early in the development process, leading to more efficient and cost-effective development.

**Types of Simulation Environments Tailored for Autonomous Systems:**

- **High-Fidelity Physics Simulators:** For agents that interact heavily with the physical world (e.g., robots, autonomous vehicles, drones), physics simulators are crucial. These sophisticated environments accurately model the dynamics of the physical environment, including gravity, friction, collisions, aerodynamics, and the realistic behavior of various sensors (e.g., cameras, lidar, radar). Examples of such simulators include Gazebo (widely used in robotics), CARLA (specifically for autonomous driving research), and SimPy (a Python-based discrete-event simulation framework that can also model continuous systems).
- **Discrete Event Simulators for Abstract Environments:** For agents operating in more abstract or event-driven environments (e.g., multi-agent systems, logistics and supply chain management, social simulations), discrete event simulators model the system as a sequence of events occurring at specific points in time. These simulators are well-suited for analyzing system-

level interactions, resource allocation, and communication patterns. Examples include SimPy and AnyLogic (a multi-method simulation software).

- **Synthetic Data Generation Tools for Perception Training and Testing:** For training and rigorously testing the perception systems of autonomous agents (e.g., object recognition, semantic segmentation), synthetic data generation tools play a vital role. These tools can create large volumes of perfectly labeled synthetic data (e.g., photorealistic images with accurate object bounding boxes and semantic labels) with precise control over various parameters such as lighting conditions, object poses, and environmental variations. This allows for targeted testing of perception algorithms under diverse and challenging conditions that might be difficult or time-consuming to capture in real-world data.

## Unit Testing of Individual Agent Components: Verifying the Building Blocks

Unit testing focuses on verifying the functional correctness of individual components or modules of the agent in complete isolation. While autonomous agents exhibit complex integrated behaviors, a well-designed modular architecture (as emphasized in Chapter 11) enables the effective unit testing of key building blocks:

- **Testing Belief State Management Modules:** Ensuring that the belief state management module correctly implements functionalities for storing, retrieving, updating, and querying the agent's internal beliefs (facts about the world and itself) under various conditions and concurrent access scenarios.

- **Testing Planning Algorithms in Isolation:** Verifying that planning algorithms (e.g., path planners, task planners) correctly generate valid and optimal (according to defined criteria) plans for a given set of initial states, goals, and environmental constraints, without relying on the actual perception or action execution modules.
- **Testing Action Selection Mechanisms:** Validating that the action selection logic correctly chooses appropriate actions based on the current state of the agent (as represented in its belief state) and its active goals, considering different action selection strategies (e.g., rule-based, utility-based).
- **Testing Perception Processing Pipelines:** Verifying the correctness of individual processing steps within the perception pipeline (e.g., sensor data filtering, noise reduction, feature extraction algorithms, object detection models) by providing them with controlled input data and asserting that they produce the expected output.
- **Strategic Use of Mock Objects and Test Stubs:** In unit testing, dependencies on other modules or the external environment are typically replaced with carefully crafted mock objects (simulating the behavior of dependent modules) and test stubs (providing controlled input data) to isolate the

component being tested and ensure that the test focuses solely on the logic of that specific unit.

## System-Level Testing of Integrated Autonomous Agents: Evaluating End-to-End Behavior

System-level testing evaluates the integrated behavior of the entire agent system and its interactions with a simulated or, in later stages, a carefully controlled real-world environment. This level of testing aims to uncover emergent issues and integration problems that might only arise when individual components are working together:

- **Integration Testing of Inter-Module Communication:** Verifying the correct and seamless interaction and communication between different modules of the agent (e.g., ensuring that the perception module correctly passes processed sensory data to the planning module, and that the planning module correctly drives the action execution module).
- **Comprehensive Scenario-Based System Testing in Simulation:** Running the fully integrated agent through a wide and diverse range of simulated scenarios, encompassing both nominal and challenging conditions, to holistically assess its overall behavior, performance, safety, and ability to achieve its goals in a simulated environment.
- **Rigorous Regression Testing for Stability:** After any modifications, bug fixes, or the introduction of new features, regression testing is

crucial to ensure that previously verified functionalities still operate correctly and that the changes haven't inadvertently introduced new issues or broken existing behavior. This is particularly important in complex autonomous systems where seemingly small changes can have unforeseen consequences in other parts of the system.

- **Carefully Controlled Real-World Testing (with Stringent Safety Protocols):** In the later stages of development and after extensive simulation testing, testing in carefully controlled and instrumented real-world environments might be necessary to validate the agent's performance, robustness, and safety in realistic physical conditions. This must be conducted with meticulous planning, strict safety protocols, comprehensive monitoring, and clearly defined fallback mechanisms.

## Introduction to Formal Verification Concepts: Mathematical Guarantees

Formal verification involves employing rigorous mathematical methods to formally prove the correctness of a system's design or implementation with respect to a precise formal specification. While the complete formal verification of highly complex autonomous agents remains a significant research challenge, certain concepts and techniques are becoming increasingly relevant, particularly for safety-critical components:

- **Precise Formal Specifications:** Defining the desired behavior and safety properties of the agent using formal mathematical languages (e.g., temporal logic, process calculi). These formal specifications provide a precise and unambiguous statement of what the system should and should not do, serving as a rigorous benchmark against which the system can be verified.
- **Automated Model Checking:** An automated verification technique that systematically explores all possible states and transitions of a finite-state system to algorithmically check if it satisfies a given formal specification (e.g., expressed in temporal logic). While computationally expensive for systems with very large state spaces, model checking can be effectively applied to verifying critical components or simplified abstract models of the agent's behavior.
- **Rigorous Theorem Proving:** Using mathematical proof techniques, often with the aid of interactive theorem provers, to formally demonstrate that the agent's design or its software implementation logically satisfies its formal specification. This approach can handle more complex and infinite-state systems than model checking but often requires significant human expertise and guidance in constructing the proofs.
- **Real-Time Runtime Verification:** Complementary to offline verification techniques, runtime verification involves continuously monitoring the execution of the agent against its formal specification in real-time. This allows for

the detection of any violations of the specified properties during the agent's operation, enabling timely intervention or safe state transitions.

Formal verification offers the potential for providing strong, mathematically grounded guarantees about the correctness and safety of autonomous systems, especially in applications where failures can have severe and unacceptable consequences. While still an active area of research, its role in ensuring the trustworthiness of highly autonomous agents is expected to grow.

**Emerging Trends in Verification and Validation for Agentic Systems:**

The field of V&V for agentic systems is rapidly evolving, with several promising emerging trends:

- **Adversarial Testing and Robustness Evaluation:** Techniques like generating adversarial examples are being adapted to test the robustness of AI-powered agents against carefully crafted inputs designed to fool them or cause undesirable behavior.
- **Explainability-Driven Validation:** Using explainability methods (as discussed in Chapter 14) to gain insights into the agent's decision-making process and identify potential flaws or biases that might not be apparent through traditional black-box testing.
- **Formal Methods Integrated with Machine Learning:** Research is exploring ways to integrate

formal verification techniques with machine learning components, for example, by formally verifying properties of learned policies or neural networks.

- **Continuous Verification and Validation (Continuous V&V):** Adopting agile and DevOps principles to implement continuous V&V processes throughout the agent's lifecycle, enabling faster feedback and more iterative improvement of reliability and safety.

Ensuring the reliability, safety, and trustworthiness of autonomous agents through rigorous verification and validation is not just a technical challenge but also a critical ethical and societal responsibility as these systems become increasingly integrated into our lives. A comprehensive and evolving approach that combines scenario-based testing, extensive simulation, unit and system-level testing, the application of formal verification concepts, and the adoption of emerging V&V trends will be essential for building and deploying agentic systems that we can confidently rely upon.

# Chapter 13

## Designing for Robustness and Fault Tolerance

As intelligent agents increasingly operate in complex, unpredictable, and often safety-critical real-world environments, their ability to maintain reliable and safe operation in the face of various challenges is paramount. **Robustness** refers to an agent's capacity to consistently maintain its performance and intended behavior despite the presence of noisy or imperfect sensory data, unexpected environmental conditions, and unforeseen interactions. **Fault tolerance**, on the other hand, focuses on an agent's ability to continue functioning correctly, or at least gracefully degrade its performance in a predictable and safe manner, even when internal hardware or software components experience failures. Designing for both robustness and fault tolerance is not merely a desirable feature but a fundamental necessity for building dependable, trustworthy, and ultimately deployable agentic systems. This chapter will delve into the core principles and practical techniques for achieving these critical qualities, with a particular emphasis on the design and implementation of effective error handling and recovery mechanisms.

**Fundamental Principles for Designing Robust Agents: Withstanding Uncertainty**

Several overarching principles should guide the design of intelligent agents that are inherently resilient to noisy data and unexpected situations:

- **Embracing Redundancy:** Incorporating redundant sensors, processing units, or algorithmic approaches can provide crucial backup and fault masking in case of a primary component failure or when inconsistencies arise between different sources of information.
- **Promoting Diversity in Approach:** Utilizing diverse algorithmic approaches for the same critical task can significantly enhance robustness. If one method encounters a limitation or is particularly susceptible to a specific type of noise or adversarial attack, another, based on a different underlying principle, might still function correctly and provide a viable alternative.
- **Designing for Graceful Degradation:** Intelligent agents should be designed to degrade their performance in a predictable, controlled, and, most importantly, safe manner when faced with challenging or off-nominal operating conditions, rather than experiencing a sudden and potentially catastrophic failure.
- **Implementing Comprehensive Error Detection:** Equipping agents with robust mechanisms for detecting anomalies, inconsistencies, or errors in their sensory input,

internal state representations, or the outcomes of their executed actions is crucial for initiating timely recovery procedures and preventing further propagation of errors.

- **Adopting Bounded Rationality and Heuristic Reasoning:** In highly complex, dynamic, or uncertain real-world situations where computational resources are limited and obtaining optimal solutions in real-time is infeasible, agents might need to rely on principles of bounded rationality and employ effective heuristic approaches. These heuristics, while not guaranteeing optimality, can often provide "good enough" solutions within acceptable time constraints and can be more robust to the inherent uncertainties of the environment than brittle, computationally intensive optimal solutions.

- **Ensuring Continuous Monitoring and Self-Assessment:** Intelligent agents should continuously monitor their own performance metrics, the quality and reliability of their sensory data streams, and the operational status of their internal hardware and software components. This proactive self-assessment allows for the early identification of potential issues, enabling the agent to take preemptive actions or trigger appropriate error handling mechanisms before a significant failure occurs.

**Practical Techniques for Enhancing Robustness: Building Resilient Agents**

A variety of practical techniques can be employed during the design and implementation phases to build more robust agentic systems:

- **Sophisticated Data Filtering and Noise Reduction:** Applying advanced signal processing techniques, statistical methods (e.g., Kalman filters, Bayesian filtering), or even deep learning-based denoising models to effectively filter out noise, outliers, and other forms of corruption from sensory data, thereby improving the accuracy and reliability of the agent's perception of the environment.
- **Strategic Sensor Fusion:** Employing intelligent sensor fusion techniques to combine data from multiple heterogeneous sensors in a way that leverages the strengths of each sensor while mitigating their individual weaknesses and noise characteristics. This can lead to a more accurate, reliable, and comprehensive understanding of the environment than can be achieved with any single sensor in isolation.
- **Principled Model Uncertainty Estimation:** For agents that rely on internal models of the environment, other agents, or their own dynamics, it is crucial to not only maintain these models but also to explicitly estimate the uncertainty associated with their predictions. This uncertainty information can then be used to inform more

robust decision-making, particularly when dealing with incomplete or noisy data, by making the agent more cautious or prompting it to gather more information.

- **Adversarial Training for Machine Learning Components:** For intelligent agents that incorporate machine learning models (e.g., for perception or control), training these models on carefully crafted adversarial examples – inputs specifically designed to fool the model – can significantly enhance their robustness to malicious attacks or unexpected perturbations in the input data that might occur in real-world scenarios.
- **Leveraging Meta-Learning for Rapid Adaptation:** Utilizing meta-learning techniques can enable agents to quickly adapt to new types of noise, sensor degradation, or unexpected situations based on their prior experience with similar challenges. By learning how to learn effectively, agents can become more resilient to novel forms of uncertainty.

**Core Principles for Designing Fault-Tolerant Agents: Maintaining Operation Amidst Failure**

Designing for fault tolerance focuses on ensuring that an agent can continue to operate, possibly with reduced functionality, even when internal components malfunction or fail:

- **Implementing Robust Fault Detection and Isolation:** Equipping the agent with mechanisms to rapidly and accurately detect when a hardware or software component has failed and to effectively isolate the faulty component to prevent the error from propagating to other critical parts of the system, thereby containing the impact of the failure.

- **Ensuring Effective Fault Containment:** Designing the agent's architecture such that the effects of a failure in one specific component are strictly contained within that module and do not cascade to other essential functionalities or critical decision-making processes of the agent. This often involves modular design with well-defined interfaces and error boundaries.
- **Strategic Use of Redundancy (Hardware and Software):** Employing redundant hardware components (e.g., backup processors, sensors, actuators, communication channels) that can seamlessly take over the functions of a primary component if it fails. Similarly, software redundancy can involve having backup algorithms, data structures, or even entire modules that can provide the same functionality in case of a primary software failure.
- **Prioritizing Graceful Degradation (Revisited):** As mentioned earlier in the context of robustness, in the event of a detected fault, a well-designed agent should aim to degrade its functionality in a controlled and safe manner, prioritizing the maintenance of essential functions and ensuring a safe state even if full performance cannot be maintained.

- **Exploring Self-Repair and Dynamic Reconfiguration:** More advanced fault-tolerant systems might incorporate mechanisms for self-diagnosing the nature and extent of a failure and potentially attempting to repair or reconfigure themselves in response. This could involve restarting a failed software component, switching to a backup hardware unit, or dynamically adjusting the agent's operational parameters.

**Designing Effective Error Handling and Recovery Mechanisms: Responding to the Inevitable**

A crucial aspect of both robustness and fault tolerance is the thoughtful design and implementation of effective error handling and recovery mechanisms that allow the agent to gracefully respond to and recover from unexpected events and component failures:

- **Proactive Error Detection and Comprehensive Reporting:** The agent should be equipped to detect a wide range of potential errors, including sensor malfunctions, communication disruptions, planning failures, execution errors, and internal software exceptions. Furthermore, it should have a robust mechanism for logging and reporting these errors internally for debugging and analysis, and potentially externally to a human operator or monitoring system.
- **Implementing Robust Exception Handling:** In the software components of the agent, well-designed exception handling mechanisms should

be in place to gracefully catch unexpected errors or exceptions that occur during program execution, preventing catastrophic crashes and allowing the agent to attempt recovery or enter a safe state.

- **Employing State Checkpointing and Rollback Strategies:** For critical tasks or operations, the agent can periodically save snapshots of its internal state (checkpointing). If an error occurs during the execution of these tasks, the agent can rollback to a previously known stable state and attempt to recover by retrying the failed operation or executing an alternative plan.
- **Implementing Intelligent Retry Mechanisms:** For transient or intermittent errors (e.g., temporary network connectivity issues, brief sensor glitches), the agent can implement intelligent retry mechanisms that automatically attempt the failed operation again after a short delay, possibly with increasing backoff times to avoid overwhelming the failing component or system.
- **Developing Pre-defined Recovery Planning:** For anticipated types of failures or common error scenarios, the agent can have pre-defined recovery plans that specify the sequence of steps to take to mitigate the impact of the failure, restore functionality, or transition to a safe operational mode. These plans might involve switching to redundant components or invoking alternative algorithms.
- **Establishing Clear Human Intervention Protocols:** In many real-world applications,

particularly those with safety-critical implications, well-defined protocols for human intervention are essential. These protocols should specify how the agent signals its inability to handle a situation or when a critical failure occurs, and how a human operator can safely monitor, intervene, diagnose problems, and potentially take over control of the agent.

**Illustrative Real-World Case Studies and Trade-offs:**

Consider the design of fly-by-wire systems in modern commercial aircraft (a critical example of a safety-critical agentic system). These systems employ triplex or even quadruplex redundancy in their flight control computers and sensors. If one computer fails, the others seamlessly take over. The system also incorporates diverse sensor types and sophisticated fault detection and isolation mechanisms. However, this level of fault tolerance comes with significant costs in terms of hardware complexity, weight, rigorous testing, and certification processes.

In contrast, consider a less safety-critical personal assistant agent. While robustness to noisy speech input is important for user experience, complete hardware redundancy for every component might be impractical due to cost constraints. The design might prioritize graceful degradation (e.g., if speech recognition fails, the agent might offer a text-based interface) and robust error reporting to the user.

As these examples illustrate, the level of robustness and fault tolerance required in an agentic system is heavily dependent on its intended application and the potential consequences of failure. Designing for these qualities often involves trade-offs between cost, complexity, performance, and the level of dependability achieved.

# Chapter 14

## Explainable Agency: Techniques and Methods

As intelligent agents evolve in complexity and permeate increasingly impactful facets of our lives, spanning domains from personalized healthcare and autonomous transportation to intricate financial modeling and critical infrastructure management, the imperative for transparency and understandability in their decision-making processes has become paramount. **Explainable AI (XAI)** emerges as a critical field dedicated to developing a suite of techniques and methodologies that empower humans to comprehend, effectively trust, and judiciously manage these sophisticated AI systems. Within the specific context of agentic systems, the ability to generate meaningful explanations is not merely an academic pursuit but a fundamental requirement for robust debugging, rigorous verification, establishing clear accountability, fostering user trust and adoption, ensuring adherence to regulatory frameworks, facilitating effective human oversight and control, and addressing crucial ethical considerations. This chapter will embark on a comprehensive exploration of both foundational and cutting-edge explainability methods specifically tailored for intelligent agents, illuminating the often-opaque reasoning behind their actions, predictions, and interactions.

## The Foundational Importance of Explainable Agency: Unveiling the Black Box

Before delving into the intricacies of specific explainability techniques, it is essential to underscore the multifaceted reasons why explainable agency is not just a desirable attribute but a fundamental necessity for the widespread and responsible deployment of intelligent agents:

- **Building Trust and Fostering Confidence:** End-users are inherently more likely to place their trust and readily adopt agents whose behavior they can readily understand and whose reasoning appears transparent and logical. This transparency cultivates a sense of confidence in the agent's reliability, competence, and alignment with user expectations and values. For instance, a user is more likely to trust a medical diagnosis agent if it can clearly articulate the factors that led to its conclusion.
- **Facilitating Debugging and Enabling Error Analysis:** When an intelligent agent makes an erroneous prediction, exhibits unexpected behavior, or fails to achieve its intended goal, the availability of clear explanations becomes invaluable for developers and operators. These explanations can serve as crucial diagnostic tools, enabling them to trace the chain of reasoning, identify the root cause of the issue (whether it lies in the data, the model, or the agent's logic), and implement targeted improvements and fixes.

- **Establishing Accountability and Assigning Responsibility:** In critical application domains where agent decisions can have significant consequences (e.g., autonomous vehicles involved in accidents, AI-powered loan approval systems denying applications), understanding the precise reasoning behind an agent's action is indispensable for establishing clear lines of accountability and assigning responsibility in the event of errors, biases, or adverse outcomes.
- **Ensuring Compliance with Regulatory Frameworks:** In an increasing number of regulated industries (e.g., finance, healthcare), regulatory bodies are mandating transparency and the provision of explanations for AI systems that make decisions impacting individuals or society. Explainability techniques are thus becoming essential for ensuring compliance with these evolving legal and ethical standards.
- **Enabling Effective Human Oversight and Control:** In many real-world deployments, particularly in semi-autonomous systems where human operators retain a degree of oversight and the potential for intervention, clear explanations of an agent's current state, its reasoning, and its intended actions are crucial for enabling informed human monitoring, timely intervention when necessary, and effective collaboration between humans and agents. For example, an air traffic control system augmented by AI needs to provide explanations for its recommendations to allow

human controllers to understand and validate them.

- **Addressing Critical Ethical Considerations:** Understanding the underlying basis of an agent's decisions is paramount for identifying and mitigating potential biases, unfairness, or discriminatory patterns that might be inadvertently embedded in the system due to biased training data or flawed algorithmic design. Explainability can thus play a vital role in ensuring the ethical and equitable deployment of intelligent agents.

- **Facilitating Knowledge Discovery and Domain Insight:** The process of generating and analyzing explanations can sometimes reveal valuable and non-obvious insights into the underlying problem domain that were not explicitly programmed into the agent. By scrutinizing the agent's reasoning, domain experts might uncover new relationships, important features, or previously overlooked patterns in the data.

## A Taxonomy of Explainability Methods: Navigating the XAI Landscape

The diverse landscape of explainability methods can be broadly categorized based on several key criteria, providing a structured way to understand their strengths, limitations, and applicability:

- **Intrinsic vs. Post-hoc Explainability:** Intrinsic methods focus on designing inherently interpretable models from the outset (e.g., rule-based systems, decision trees), where the model's structure directly lends itself to explanation. Post-hoc methods, in contrast, are applied to already trained "black-box" models (e.g., deep neural networks) to generate explanations after the fact.

- **Model-Specific vs. Model-Agnostic Explainability:** Model-specific methods are tailored to the specific architecture and internal workings of a particular type of model (e.g., attention mechanisms in transformers, feature importance in linear models). Model-agnostic methods, conversely, are designed to be applicable to a wide range of different model types, treating them as black boxes and focusing on the relationship between their inputs and outputs.
- **Local vs. Global Explainability:** Local explanations aim to provide insights into the reasoning behind a single, specific prediction or decision made by the agent for a particular input instance. Global explanations, on the other hand, strive to provide an overall understanding of the agent's general behavior and the relationships it has learned between input features and outputs across the entire input space.

## Basic Explainability Methods: Inherently Transparent Approaches

These foundational methods often yield more direct, intuitive, and human-understandable explanations due to their inherent simplicity and transparent structure:

168

- **Rule-Based Systems:** Intelligent agents built upon explicitly defined sets of rules (e.g., a collection of "if-then-else" statements) are inherently interpretable. The reasoning behind a specific decision or action can be directly traced back to the particular rule or chain of rules that were triggered by the current input state.
- **Decision Trees:** Decision tree models provide a hierarchical, tree-like structure of sequential decisions based on the values of input features. Each path from the root of the tree down to a leaf node, which represents the final prediction or classification, offers a clear and intuitive explanation of the decision-making process based on a series of logical conditions.
- **Linear Models with Interpretable Feature Importance:** In linear models such as linear regression and logistic regression, the learned coefficients associated with each input feature directly indicate the feature's importance and the direction (positive or negative) of its influence on the model's prediction. These coefficients can serve as a form of global explanation, revealing which features the model deems most significant in making its decisions.

**Advanced Explainability Methods: Peering Inside the Black Box**

These more sophisticated techniques are often employed to shed light on the inner workings of complex, "black-box" models like deep neural networks, providing insights into their reasoning processes:

- **Attention Mechanisms:** In neural network architectures, particularly sequence-to-sequence models and transformers, attention mechanisms enable the model to selectively focus on the most relevant parts of the input data when making a prediction or taking an action. The learned attention weights assigned to different input elements (e.g., words in a sentence, spatial regions in an image) can be visualized to understand which parts of the input the model deemed most important for its decision.
- **Saliency Maps and Gradient-Based Methods:** For image-based deep learning models, saliency maps are visualization techniques that highlight the regions or pixels in the input image that have the most significant influence on the model's classification or prediction. Methods like Grad-CAM (Gradient-weighted Class Activation Mapping) and SmoothGrad use the gradients of the output with respect to the input image to generate these saliency maps, providing a visual explanation of what the model "sees" as important.
- **Rule Extraction from Black-Box Models:** A class of techniques aims to extract human-understandable rules or decision sets from complex, pre-trained black-box models. These extracted rules can then serve as more interpretable approximations of the model's behavior, providing a way to understand its

decision boundaries in a symbolic form. Methods include inducing decision trees from the black-box model's input-output pairs and using symbolic regression to find mathematical expressions that approximate the model's function.

- **Counterfactual Explanations:** Counterfactual explanations address the question "What if things had been different?". For a given prediction or decision, they identify the smallest set of changes to the input features that would have resulted in a different, often desired, outcome. This can help users understand which factors need to be altered to achieve a specific result. For example, a counterfactual explanation for a loan application denial might be: "If your income had been $5,000 higher, your loan would have been approved."

- **SHAP (SHapley Additive exPlanations):** SHAP is a model-agnostic, post-hoc method rooted in game theory that aims to explain the output of any machine learning model by assigning each input feature an importance value (Shapley value) for a particular prediction. These values quantify the contribution of each feature to the difference between the actual prediction and the average prediction across [1] the dataset. SHAP provides both local explanations (for individual predictions) and global explanations (by aggregating local feature importances).

- **LIME (Local Interpretable Model-agnostic Explanations):** LIME is another powerful model-agnostic, post-hoc technique that seeks to explain the predictions of any classifier or regressor by approximating the complex black-box model locally around the specific instance being explained with a more interpretable model, such as a linear model or a decision tree. LIME generates explanations by perturbing the input data point, getting predictions from the black-box model for these perturbed samples, and then fitting a simple, interpretable model to these local samples, using the weights or structure of this local model as the explanation for the original prediction.

- **Causal Inference Methods for Explainability:** Some of the most advanced and promising explainability approaches leverage techniques from causal inference to move beyond mere correlations and attempt to understand the true causal relationships between input features and the agent's decisions. By identifying causal pathways, these methods can provide deeper, more actionable, and potentially more robust explanations. Examples include using structural causal models and intervention analysis to understand the effect of changing specific input features on the agent's output.

## Applying Explainability to Diverse Agent Components: Understanding the Inner Workings

The aforementioned explainability techniques can be strategically applied to various internal components of an intelligent agent to gain a deeper understanding of their specific contributions to the overall behavior:

- **Perception Modules:** Understanding why an agent perceives its environment in a particular way (e.g., why it detected a specific object, misidentified a scene). Techniques like attention mechanisms (for vision transformers) and saliency maps can highlight the input features that were most influential in the perception process.
- **Belief State Management:** Explaining why the agent holds certain beliefs about the world, other agents, or itself (e.g., based on specific sensory inputs, inferences drawn from past experiences, or communicated information). Tracing back the chain of evidence and the reasoning steps that led to the formation or updating of a belief can provide valuable explanations.
- **Planning Modules:** Understanding the rationale behind a chosen plan of action (e.g., the specific goals the plan aims to achieve, the reasons for selecting a particular sequence of actions over alternatives). Visualizing the generated plan, along with the estimated utilities or costs associated with different actions and states, can offer insights into the planner's decision-making process.
- **Action Selection Mechanisms:** Explaining why a specific action was chosen by the agent in a given state (e.g., based on a learned policy in reinforcement learning, a utility function in a decision-theoretic agent, or a set of prioritized rules). Examining the feature importance derived from the learned policy or the utility values

assigned to different possible actions can provide explanations.

- **Communication Modules (in Multi-Agent Systems or Human-Agent Interaction):** Understanding the intent and reasoning behind a communicated message from the agent (e.g., in a multi-agent negotiation or a human-chatbot interaction). Analyzing the underlying goals, beliefs, and communicative strategies driving the message generation process is key to providing meaningful explanations.

**Challenges and Future Directions in Explainable Agency for Intelligent Systems**

Despite the significant advancements in the field of explainable AI, generating effective and meaningful explanations for increasingly complex intelligent agents still presents several key challenges and motivates ongoing research:

- **The Inherent Trade-off between Accuracy and Interpretability:** Often, more complex and powerful models (e.g., deep neural networks) achieve higher levels of accuracy on challenging tasks but are inherently less transparent and harder to interpret than simpler models (e.g., linear models, decision trees). Finding the optimal balance between predictive performance and the interpretability of the agent's reasoning remains a critical challenge.

- **Ensuring the Faithfulness of Explanations:** A crucial concern is whether the generated explanations truly reflect the actual reasoning process of the underlying model or agent, or if they are merely providing superficial correlations or post-hoc rationalizations. Ensuring the faithfulness and fidelity of explanations is essential for building trust and enabling effective debugging.
- **The Critical Need for User-Centricity:** Explanations need to be tailored to the specific background, knowledge, and needs of the intended user. Different stakeholders (e.g., developers, end-users, domain experts, regulatory bodies) will likely require different types, levels of detail, and formats of explanations. Designing user-centric explanation interfaces and methodologies is an active area of research.
- **Scaling Explainability to Complex Agents and Environments:** Generating meaningful and actionable explanations for intelligent agents operating in very large state and action spaces or interacting within highly complex and dynamic environments remains a significant technical hurdle. Many current XAI methods struggle to scale effectively to such scenarios.
- **Developing Robust Metrics for Evaluating Explanation Quality:** Establishing objective and reliable metrics for evaluating the quality, completeness, understandability, and trustworthiness of generated explanations is an ongoing and challenging area of research. How do

we quantitatively measure if an explanation is "good"?

- **Seamlessly Integrating Explainability into the Agent's Architecture:** A promising future direction involves designing agent architectures that inherently support explainability from the ground up, rather than treating it as an afterthought. This could involve incorporating interpretable components or designing the learning and reasoning processes in a way that naturally lends itself to explanation.
- **Explaining Sequences of Decisions and Behaviors:** Since intelligent agents often engage in sequential decision-making and exhibit complex behaviors over time, developing methods to explain these sequences of actions and the underlying temporal dependencies is a crucial area for future research.

# Chapter 15

# Human-in-the-Loop Control and Oversight

As intelligent agents increasingly demonstrate advanced capabilities and are deployed across a spectrum of complex and often safety-critical domains – ranging from autonomous vehicles navigating public roads and robotic assistants performing delicate surgical procedures to sophisticated AI systems managing critical infrastructure and making high-stakes financial decisions – the design of systems that seamlessly and effectively integrate human monitoring, intervention, and nuanced guidance becomes not just advantageous but absolutely paramount. The principles of **Human-in-the-Loop (HITL)** control and oversight are rooted in the understanding that the synergistic collaboration between the unique strengths of human operators (such as common sense reasoning, adaptability to genuinely novel and unforeseen situations, nuanced ethical and moral judgment, and the capacity for holistic understanding) and the computational prowess of intelligent agents (including their speed, efficiency in processing vast amounts of data, consistency in execution, and ability to operate in hazardous environments) can lead to the creation of more reliable, demonstrably safer, and ultimately more trustworthy and ethically aligned systems. This chapter will delve into a comprehensive exploration of various crucial strategies for designing such effective HITL systems, with a particular emphasis on their application in critical domains where the consequences of system error or failure can be severe. Furthermore, we will critically examine the significant and evolving ethical considerations that inevitably arise with the increasing levels of autonomy afforded to these intelligent agents and the shifting roles of their human counterparts.

**Strategies for Human-in-the-Loop Design: Orchestrating Human-Agent Collaboration**

Designing truly effective HITL systems necessitates a meticulous and human-centered approach, requiring careful consideration of the distinct roles and responsibilities allocated to both human operators and autonomous agents, as well as the intuitive interfaces and robust mechanisms that seamlessly facilitate their interaction and collaboration:

- **Defining Appropriate Levels of Automation:** A foundational aspect of HITL design involves thoughtfully determining and clearly defining the most appropriate level of automation for each specific task or sub-task within the overall system operation. This exists along a continuous spectrum, ranging from fully manual control entirely executed by a human operator to fully autonomous operation where the agent makes all decisions and acts independently. In between these extremes lie various crucial levels of shared control and intelligent human assistance. A widely recognized framework for understanding this spectrum is Sheridan's Levels of Automation, which provides a detailed categorization of the degree to which a computer system recommends, selects, executes, and ultimately ignores human input in the decision-making and action execution processes.

- **Ensuring Effective Monitoring and Comprehensive Situation Awareness:** Designing intuitive and informative interfaces and providing human operators with the necessary data and visualizations to maintain a high level of situation awareness regarding the agent's current state, the dynamics of its operational environment, and its progress toward achieving its designated goals is absolutely critical. This includes the effective visualization of raw and processed sensor data, the agent's internal states and beliefs, its planned future actions, and any potential risks or uncertainties it has identified. Maintaining a comprehensive and up-to-date understanding of the overall situation is paramount for enabling timely and effective human intervention when required.

- **Providing Clear and Intuitive Mechanisms for Human Intervention:** HITL systems must incorporate clear, reliable, and intuitively designed mechanisms that allow human operators to intervene in the agent's ongoing operation when deemed necessary. This can encompass a range of capabilities, including the ability to temporarily pause the agent's current task, modify its overarching goals or specific sub-goals, adjust critical operational parameters, directly override the agent's autonomous decisions, or even take full manual control of the system. The design of these intervention mechanisms must carefully consider factors such as latency (the delay between human input and system response), inherent safety implications of intervention, and the potential cognitive load imposed on the human operator during high-pressure situations.

- **Facilitating Guidance and Seamless Collaboration:** Effective HITL design also involves creating systems that allow human operators to provide high-level guidance, offer specific constraints, and engage in genuine collaborative planning with the autonomous agent. This might involve a human operator specifying broad mission objectives, defining forbidden zones or operational boundaries, offering suggestions based on their expert knowledge, or jointly selecting a sequence of tasks or waypoints with the agent. The agent, in turn, should be designed to effectively understand, interpret, and seamlessly incorporate this human input into its decision-making and action planning processes.

- **Achieving Appropriate Trust Calibration:** Designing the system and providing consistent and transparent feedback on the agent's performance, capabilities, and inherent limitations is crucial for helping human operators develop an appropriately calibrated level of trust. Over-trust in a seemingly infallible system can lead to dangerous complacency and a failure to intervene when the agent encounters situations it cannot handle correctly. Conversely, under-trust can result in unnecessary and potentially disruptive interventions, hindering the agent's efficiency and the overall system performance.

- **Integrating Explainability for Informed Oversight:** The seamless integration of explainability techniques (as thoroughly discussed in Chapter 14) is paramount for providing human operators with meaningful insights into the agent's underlying reasoning and decision-making processes. Understanding *why* an agent is taking a particular course of action, especially in complex or critical situations, is absolutely crucial for enabling informed monitoring, effective intervention, and the development of appropriate trust.
- **Providing Comprehensive Training and Skill Development:** The effectiveness of any HITL system is heavily reliant on the adequate training and skill development of the human operators who are tasked with monitoring, interacting with, and potentially intervening in the agent's operation. This training must encompass a thorough understanding of the agent's capabilities, its inherent limitations, the established procedures for different levels of human-agent interaction, and best practices for effective monitoring and timely intervention in both nominal and off-nominal scenarios.
- **Implementing Adaptive Automation for Optimized Performance:** Designing systems that

possess the capability to dynamically adjust the level of automation employed for different tasks based on a variety of real-time factors, such as the complexity of the current situation, the agent's level of confidence in its own assessment, and the human operator's current workload and availability, can significantly enhance overall system performance and safety. This adaptive automation ensures that the right level of human or agent control is applied at the most appropriate time.

## Human-in-the-Loop in Critical Applications: Ensuring Safety and Reliability

In high-stakes domains where the consequences of even a single agent error or system failure can be catastrophic – such as autonomous surgery performing intricate procedures, air traffic control managing the safe flow of aircraft, or AI systems overseeing the operation of nuclear power plants – the design and implementation of robust and rigorously tested HITL strategies are not merely best practices but fundamental safety imperatives:

- **Employing Supervisory Control Architectures:** In many critical applications, human operators often adopt a supervisory role, setting high-level goals, defining operational constraints, and monitoring the agent's overall progress. The autonomous agent then manages the lower-level details of task execution, with human intervention typically reserved for exceptional circumstances, detected anomalies, or when the agent explicitly requests human guidance or confirmation.

- **Developing Shared Control Architectures with Clear Authority:** Architectures where control authority is explicitly shared between the human operator and the autonomous agent, with each having primary responsibility over specific aspects of the task or the ability to influence the overall system behavior, require carefully designed coordination and robust conflict resolution mechanisms to ensure safe and coherent operation.

- **Implementing Reliable and Readily Accessible Human Override Capabilities:** In virtually all safety-critical agentic systems, the provision of a reliable, intuitive, and immediately accessible mechanism for a human operator to directly override the agent's autonomous actions and take full manual control is a fundamental safety requirement. These override systems must be designed with the highest levels of reliability and must be easily activated in emergency situations.

- **Facilitating Effective Multi-Operator Coordination:** Complex critical systems may necessitate the involvement of multiple human operators, each overseeing different aspects of the agent's operation or collaborating on complex interventions. Designing clear communication protocols, shared situational awareness displays, and coordinated control mechanisms is essential for ensuring effective teamwork in these scenarios.

- **Conducting Extensive Scenario-Based Training and Simulation:** Comprehensive and realistic training in simulated operational environments, encompassing both routine scenarios and a wide range of potential failure conditions and emergency situations, is absolutely crucial for adequately preparing human operators to effectively monitor, interact with, and intervene in critical autonomous systems. These simulations allow operators to develop the necessary skills and mental models without risking real-world consequences.

## Ethical Considerations of Autonomy and Human Oversight: Navigating the Moral Landscape

The increasing levels of autonomy afforded to intelligent agents inevitably raise profound and multifaceted ethical considerations, particularly concerning the evolving roles of human operators and the very nature of responsibility and control:

- **Determining Responsibility and Liability in Autonomous Systems:** As agents become more independent in their decision-making and actions, the question of who bears responsibility and legal liability in the event of errors, accidents, or unintended consequences becomes increasingly complex and requires careful legal and ethical consideration. The degree of human control and oversight retained in the system plays a crucial role in these complex determinations.

- **Balancing Trust and Avoiding Over-Reliance:** While fostering appropriate trust in the capabilities of autonomous systems is essential for their effective utilization, it is equally critical to guard against the development of over-reliance, which can lead to human operators becoming complacent, failing to adequately monitor the system's behavior, and being ill-prepared to intervene effectively when necessary.
- **Addressing the Potential for Deskilling of Human Operators:** Over-dependence on highly automated systems over extended periods might inadvertently lead to a gradual degradation of human operators' fundamental skills and abilities to perform critical tasks manually in the event of a complete system failure or in situations requiring nuanced human judgment that the agent may lack.
- **Mitigating the "Out-of-the-Loop" Problem:** When human operators primarily assume the role of passive monitors, intervening only infrequently, their overall situation awareness can significantly degrade over time. This "out-of-the-loop" phenomenon can make it substantially more difficult for them to effectively and safely take control of the system when a critical situation demands immediate human intervention.
- **Identifying and Mitigating Bias and Ensuring Fairness:** Autonomous agents are susceptible to inheriting and even amplifying biases present in the data they are trained on. Human oversight, coupled with robust explainability mechanisms that allow humans to understand the agent's

reasoning, can play a crucial role in identifying and actively mitigating these potentially harmful biases and ensuring fairer outcomes.

- **Upholding Transparency and the Ethical Imperative of Explainability:** From a fundamental ethical standpoint, particularly in the context of agent decisions that have significant impacts on individuals or society, there is a compelling moral argument for designing autonomous agents that can provide clear, understandable, and faithful explanations for their reasoning and actions. Transparency fosters trust, enables accountability, and facilitates human oversight.

- **Striving for Alignment with Human Values and Ethical Principles:** A significant and ongoing challenge lies in designing autonomous agents whose behavior is consistently aligned with fundamental human values and evolving ethical principles. Human oversight, the ability for humans to provide guidance and feedback on the agent's behavior, and the incorporation of ethical considerations into the agent's design are crucial for steering agent behavior in ethically desirable directions.

- **Addressing the Potential for Misuse of Autonomous Capabilities:** The very capabilities that make autonomous agents so powerful also carry the inherent risk of potential misuse for unintended or even malicious purposes. Robust human control and oversight mechanisms, coupled with clear ethical guidelines, stringent regulations, and proactive security measures, are necessary to mitigate these significant risks.

Designing effective human-in-the-loop control and oversight strategies is not merely a technical challenge but a fundamental prerequisite for responsibly and safely harnessing the immense potential of intelligent agents, particularly in critical applications. Furthermore, a deep and ongoing consideration of the profound ethical implications of increasing autonomy and the evolving role of human involvement is absolutely crucial for building trustworthy, ethically sound, and ultimately beneficial agentic systems that truly serve humanity's best interests.

# Part 5

## Advanced Topics and Future Directions

**Advanced Topics and Future Directions** delves into the cutting edge of Agentic AI. We will begin by exploring **Hybrid Agent Architectures**, examining how symbolic and sub-symbolic AI can be integrated for enhanced reasoning and learning. Next, we'll provide **Practical Guidance on Integrating Agents with Existing Ecosystems**, covering deployment and connectivity with various software and hardware infrastructures. We will then engage in an **In-depth Discussion of Ethical Considerations in Agentic AI**, focusing on the profound implications of highly autonomous systems. Finally, we will look towards **The Future of Agentic AI: Emerging Trends**, exploring potential advancements and research directions shaping the field.

# Chapter 16

## Hybrid Agent Architectures

The ongoing quest to create truly intelligent agents capable of navigating the complexities and nuances of the real world has increasingly led researchers and practitioners to explore architectures that transcend the traditional dichotomy between symbolic and sub-symbolic Artificial Intelligence. Symbolic AI, with its foundation in explicit knowledge representation through symbols, rules, and logical inference, has long been lauded for its capacity for interpretable reasoning, planning, and manipulation of abstract concepts. Conversely, sub-symbolic AI, encompassing the powerful realm of machine learning, neural networks, and connectionist models, has demonstrated remarkable prowess in learning intricate patterns directly from raw data, excelling in tasks such as perception, robust pattern recognition, and the approximation of complex functions.

The emergence of **hybrid agent architectures** signifies a paradigm shift towards synergistic integration, recognizing that the limitations inherent in relying solely on either symbolic or sub-symbolic approaches can be potentially overcome by creating intelligent agents that seamlessly leverage the complementary strengths of both. The overarching goal is to engineer systems that exhibit enhanced reasoning and learning capabilities, leading to agents that are more robust, adaptable, explainable, and ultimately more effective in tackling the multifaceted challenges of real-world intelligence. This chapter will delve into a comprehensive exploration of various advanced architectural paradigms that aim to achieve this seamless integration of symbolic and sub-symbolic AI.

## Revisiting the Dichotomy: Strengths and Weaknesses in Isolation

To fully appreciate the compelling motivations behind the development of hybrid architectures, it is crucial to briefly revisit and critically examine the inherent strengths and weaknesses that characterize both the symbolic and sub-symbolic AI paradigms when employed in isolation:

**Symbolic AI:**

- **Inherent Strengths:** Symbolic AI shines in its capacity for **interpretability**, where the agent's reasoning processes are often transparent and can be explicitly traced back to the specific rules, facts, and logical inferences that led to a particular decision or action. It exhibits strong capabilities in **logical reasoning**, making it well-suited for tasks demanding deductive inference, structured planning, and problem-solving based on explicitly encoded knowledge. Furthermore, symbolic approaches provide effective mechanisms for **knowledge representation**, allowing for the encoding and manipulation of structured information and the relationships between different concepts. Finally, symbolic AI can effectively deal with **abstract concepts and high-**

level **reasoning**, operating on symbolic representations that abstract away from the raw sensory details.

- **Inherent Weaknesses:** However, symbolic AI often suffers from **brittleness**, where its performance can degrade significantly and unpredictably when confronted with novel, ambiguous, or unexpected situations that are not explicitly covered by its predefined rules or knowledge base. The **knowledge acquisition bottleneck** presents another significant challenge, as the process of manually acquiring, formalizing, and encoding the necessary domain knowledge can be an extremely time-consuming, labor-intensive, and expertise-dependent undertaking. Moreover, symbolic systems typically exhibit **difficulty with perception and learning directly from raw data**, lacking the inherent mechanisms to process messy sensory inputs or learn complex patterns from large datasets without explicit symbolic pre-processing. Lastly, they can demonstrate a **lack of robustness to noise and uncertainty** in the input data, often requiring clean and unambiguous symbolic representations for effective operation.

## Sub-Symbolic AI:

- **Inherent Strengths:** In stark contrast, sub-symbolic AI excels at **learning complex patterns and representations directly from vast amounts of data**, without requiring explicit symbolic encoding. This data-driven approach often leads to **robustness to noise and uncertainty** in the input, as the learned representations can be more resilient to minor variations and imperfections. Sub-symbolic methods have achieved remarkable success in **perception and pattern recognition** tasks, including image and speech recognition, natural language understanding, and sensory data processing. Furthermore, these systems possess the inherent capability for **adaptability**, allowing them to improve their performance over time as they are exposed to more data and refined through learning algorithms.

- **Inherent Weaknesses:** A significant limitation of many sub-symbolic approaches, particularly deep neural networks, is the **lack of transparency and interpretability** in their reasoning processes. The complex, distributed representations learned within these models often make it extremely difficult to understand *why* a particular decision was made, hindering debugging, trust-building, and accountability. Sub-symbolic AI can also struggle with **abstract reasoning and symbolic manipulation**, often lacking the explicit mechanisms for logical deduction and planning based on symbolic knowledge. Their performance is heavily **data-dependent**, requiring large, high-quality training datasets to achieve optimal results, and they are susceptible to learning and perpetuating **biases** present within that training data.

## The Compelling Motivations for Hybrid Architectures: Bridging the Divide

The inherent limitations of relying solely on either the structured logic of symbolic AI or the data-driven pattern recognition of sub-symbolic AI when attempting to tackle the full spectrum of complex, real-world problems have served as the primary impetus behind the burgeoning field of hybrid agent architectures. The key motivations driving this integration include:

- **Synergistically Combining Strengths:** The fundamental goal is to create agents that can harness the explicit interpretability and robust logical reasoning capabilities of symbolic AI in concert with the powerful learning abilities and inherent robustness to noise and uncertainty exhibited by sub-symbolic AI.
- **Effectively Overcoming Inherent Weaknesses:** Hybrid approaches offer the potential to mitigate the brittleness often associated with purely symbolic systems by incorporating data-driven learning mechanisms that allow for adaptation to novel situations. Conversely, they can address the "black box" problem of sub-symbolic systems by integrating symbolic reasoning layers or using symbolic methods to generate explanations for sub-symbolic decisions.
- **Enabling Agents to Tackle Truly Complex Tasks:** Many real-world tasks demand both high-level abstract reasoning and low-level perception and control. Hybrid architectures aim to equip

agents with the multifaceted capabilities required for domains such as autonomous driving in unpredictable environments, sophisticated robotics operating in unstructured settings, and advanced natural language understanding and complex dialogue systems.

- **Achieving Enhanced Robustness and Adaptability:** By integrating learning from data with explicit knowledge and logical constraints, hybrid agents can potentially achieve greater resilience when faced with novel or unexpected situations and can adapt their behavior through ongoing learning while still adhering to logical principles and leveraging their encoded knowledge.

## Diverse Types of Hybrid Agent Architectures: A Spectrum of Integration

The integration of symbolic and sub-symbolic AI in agent architectures has been explored through a variety of innovative approaches, which can be broadly categorized based on the degree of coupling between the two paradigms and the directionality of information flow:

- **Loosely Coupled Architectures: Modular Collaboration:** In these architectures, the symbolic and sub-symbolic components operate as relatively independent modules that communicate with each other through well-defined and often symbolic interfaces. For instance, a sophisticated sub-symbolic perception system, such as a deep convolutional neural network, might process raw sensory data (e.g., images, audio) and then output symbolic descriptions of the perceived environment (e.g., "detected a pedestrian at location (x, y) with 98% confidence") to a separate symbolic planning system that then uses this information to reason about and plan the agent's subsequent actions.

- **Tightly Coupled Architectures: Deep Integration:** These architectures involve a much deeper and more intertwined interaction between the symbolic and sub-symbolic components, often with information flowing bidirectionally and representations being directly shared or transformed between the two levels of processing:
  - **Semantic Perception: Bridging Sensory Input to Symbolic Meaning:** A key aspect of tight coupling involves designing sub-symbolic perception systems that are specifically trained to directly output symbolic representations of the perceived world, often along with associated confidence levels or probabilities. This directly bridges the gap between raw sensory input and the symbolic knowledge that can be used for reasoning and planning. For example, a semantic perception module might take a raw image as input and output a structured symbolic representation like "Object(type=car, color=red, location=(10, 20), confidence=0.95)".

- Neural-Symbolic Integration: **Embedding Symbols within Networks:** This category of tight coupling focuses on embedding symbolic structures and explicit reasoning processes directly within the architecture of neural networks, or conversely, using neural networks to learn how to effectively represent and manipulate symbolic information. Examples include neural networks designed to perform logical inference based on knowledge graphs or architectures that incorporate symbolic rules as constraints during the learning process.
  - **Neuro-Symbolic AI Systems: Bidirectional Information Exchange:** The most deeply integrated neuro-symbolic AI systems aim for a truly bidirectional and synergistic relationship between neural network components and symbolic knowledge/reasoning modules. In these architectures, neural networks can learn and refine symbolic knowledge and reasoning rules from data, while symbolic structures and explicit knowledge can, in turn, guide and constrain the learning process within the neural networks, leading to more robust and interpretable learning.
- **Hybrid Control Architectures: Symbolic Planning, Sub-Symbolic Execution:** These

architectures specifically focus on combining the strengths of symbolic planning and high-level decision-making with the adaptability and low-level control capabilities learned through sub-symbolic methods like reinforcement learning or imitation learning. A symbolic planner might generate abstract, high-level plans or sequences of goals, while a sub-symbolic controller, trained through learning, handles the complex, continuous low-level actions required to execute these plans in a dynamic environment, often adapting to unforeseen circumstances.

## Illustrative Examples of Hybrid Agent Architectures in Action

The principles of hybrid agent architectures are exemplified in a growing number of notable systems and research directions:

- **Classic Cognitive Architectures (SOAR & CLARION):** Architectures like SOAR (State Operator And Result) have long aimed to integrate symbolic reasoning based on problem spaces, operators, and production rules with various learning mechanisms, including chunking for acquiring new rules from problem-solving experiences. CLARION (Cognitive Architecture for Integrated Intelligent Agents) explicitly models the interaction between implicit (sub-symbolic, associative learning) and explicit (symbolic, rule-based reasoning) cognitive processes.

- **Deep Reinforcement Learning with Symbolic Planning (e.g., AlphaGo & Beyond):** While primarily rooted in deep reinforcement learning (a sub-symbolic approach), DeepMind's groundbreaking systems like AlphaGo and AlphaZero for playing complex games also incorporate elements of symbolic reasoning and search in the form of Monte Carlo Tree Search (MCTS) to guide exploration and select promising moves based on strategic evaluation. Subsequent research has further explored tighter integrations of symbolic planning with deep reinforcement learning for more complex tasks.

- **Neuro-Symbolic Visual Reasoning for Question Answering:** A significant area of research involves using neural networks to process visual input (e.g., images, videos) and extract structured symbolic representations (e.g., objects, attributes, relationships) that are then fed into symbolic reasoning engines to answer complex questions about the visual scene.

- **Advanced Robotics Architectures for Complex Manipulation and Navigation:** Many contemporary robotics architectures designed for operating in unstructured and dynamic environments integrate high-level symbolic task planning (e.g., using task and motion planning algorithms) with low-level sub-symbolic control policies learned through techniques like reinforcement learning, imitation learning, or dynamic movement primitives, enabling robots to perform complex manipulation tasks and navigate intricate spaces.

- **Hybrid Approaches in Natural Language Understanding and Dialogue:** Research in natural language processing increasingly explores hybrid models that combine the statistical power of deep learning for understanding the nuances of language with symbolic knowledge bases and logical reasoning for tasks like question answering, common-sense reasoning, and engaging in more coherent and informative dialogues.

## Key Challenges and Promising Future Directions

Despite the significant progress in the field, the development of truly seamless and effective hybrid agent architectures still presents several fundamental challenges that drive ongoing and future research:

- **Bridging the Inherent Representation Gap:** One of the most significant hurdles is effectively translating information and representations between the continuous, distributed representations learned by sub-symbolic models and the discrete, structured representations used in symbolic systems without significant loss of information or misinterpretation during the conversion process.
- **Orchestrating the Interaction and Control Flow:** Determining the optimal mechanisms and

strategies for how the symbolic and sub-symbolic components should interact, influence each other's processing, and contribute to the overall decision-making and behavior of the agent remains a complex design challenge.

- **Automated Learning of Symbolic Knowledge from Sub-Symbolic Data:** A crucial area of research focuses on developing methods that can automatically extract meaningful and generalizable symbolic rules, facts, and relationships from the patterns and representations learned by sub-symbolic models, effectively making "black boxes" more transparent and contributing to symbolic knowledge acquisition.

- **Principled Injection of Symbolic Knowledge into Sub-Symbolic Learning:** Conversely, finding effective and principled ways to incorporate explicit symbolic knowledge, constraints, and reasoning principles into the learning process of sub-symbolic models is essential for improving their robustness, guiding their learning towards more meaningful representations, and potentially reducing the need for massive amounts of training data.

- **Robust Reasoning with Uncertainty in Integrated Systems:** Hybrid systems must be able to effectively handle the inherent uncertainty associated with the outputs of sub-symbolic components (e.g., probabilistic predictions from neural networks) within the more deterministic frameworks of symbolic reasoning, allowing for robust decision-making in the face of ambiguity.

- **Developing Unified Theoretical Frameworks for Hybrid Intelligence:** The field would benefit significantly from the development of more general and unified theoretical frameworks that can provide a deeper understanding of the principles underlying effective hybrid intelligence and offer guidance for the design and analysis of such integrated architectures.

Future research in hybrid agent architectures is poised to focus on addressing these critical challenges and exploring novel approaches to achieve even deeper and more synergistic integration of symbolic and sub-symbolic AI. This includes exciting advancements in areas like neural-symbolic computation, innovative methods for learning interpretable symbolic representations from neural networks, and the continued development of sophisticated cognitive architectures that naturally and seamlessly blend symbolic and sub-symbolic processing to create more robust, adaptable, and inherently explainable intelligent agents capable of tackling the full complexity of real-world intelligence.

The continued evolution and refinement of hybrid agent architectures hold immense promise for unlocking the next generation of intelligent systems, capable of exhibiting both sophisticated reasoning and robust learning, ultimately leading to more capable and trustworthy AI agents.

# Chapter 17

## Integrating Agents with Existing Ecosystems

The true transformative potential of intelligent agents is often unlocked when they can seamlessly and securely interact with and intelligently augment the vast landscape of existing technological infrastructure. The practicalities of deploying and connecting agentic AI to established software platforms (ranging from enterprise-level systems to specialized applications), a diverse array of cloud services (encompassing compute, storage, and AI/ML capabilities), resource-constrained edge devices, and the expansive and interconnected infrastructure of the Internet of Things (IoT) present both remarkable opportunities for innovation and considerable technical and architectural challenges. Effective and well-designed integration is absolutely crucial for leveraging the wealth of data, the diverse functionalities, and the distributed computational resources available within these heterogeneous ecosystems to build truly practical, scalable, and impactful agentic applications that can address real-world problems. This chapter will provide comprehensive and practical guidance on the key considerations, architectural patterns, and essential techniques involved in achieving this critical integration.

**Overarching Considerations for Seamless Integration**

Before delving into the specifics of technologies and integration approaches tailored to different types of ecosystems, several overarching considerations must guide the strategic planning and execution of any agentic AI integration effort:

- **Clearly Defining Specific Integration Goals:** The integration process must be driven by clearly articulated and well-defined goals. What precise functionalities or specific data access is required from the existing ecosystem to enable the agent to perform its intended tasks effectively? A lack of clarity at this stage can lead to inefficient integration efforts and a failure to realize the desired benefits.
- **Achieving a Deep Understanding of Ecosystem Architecture:** A thorough and granular understanding of the underlying architecture, the available Application Programming Interfaces (APIs), the prevailing data formats, and the standard communication protocols of the target software platforms, cloud services, edge devices, and IoT infrastructure is absolutely essential. This knowledge forms the bedrock upon which successful integration strategies are built.
- **Prioritizing Robust Security and Data Privacy:** Integrating with external systems inherently introduces potential security vulnerabilities and raises significant data privacy concerns. Implementing robust and multi-layered

authentication mechanisms, granular authorization controls, end-to-end data encryption both in transit and at rest, and adherence to relevant security best practices are paramount.

- **Designing for Optimal Scalability and Performance:** The integration architecture must be carefully designed to handle the anticipated data volumes, transaction rates, and user concurrency without creating performance bottlenecks that impede the agent's responsiveness or the stability of the connected systems. Scalability should be a key design principle from the outset.

- **Ensuring High Reliability and Robust Fault Tolerance:** The integrated system should be designed to be resilient to potential failures in any of the connected components. Implementing comprehensive error handling mechanisms, intelligent retry strategies, circuit breaker patterns, and well-defined fallback procedures is crucial for maintaining system availability and data integrity.

- **Planning for Long-Term Maintainability and Seamless Upgradability:** The integration solution should be architected with ease of maintenance in mind, allowing for efficient updates, patching, and modifications over time. It should also be designed to accommodate future upgrades and changes in both the agent's internal logic and the APIs or functionalities of the connected ecosystems without causing significant disruptions.

- **Leveraging Interoperability and Adhering to Open Standards:** Where feasible and appropriate, favoring the use of open standards, widely adopted data formats, and interoperable technologies can significantly simplify the integration process, reduce vendor lock-in, and enhance the long-term flexibility and portability of the agentic system.
- **Careful Consideration of Cost and Resource Management:** The total cost of integration, encompassing development efforts, deployment expenses, ongoing maintenance overhead, and the consumption of computational resources (CPU, memory, network bandwidth), should be meticulously evaluated and managed throughout the lifecycle of the integrated agentic system.

**Seamless Integration with Software Platforms and Cloud Services**

A significant number of agentic applications will necessitate seamless interaction with existing enterprise software platforms (such as Enterprise Resource Planning (ERP) systems, Customer Relationship Management (CRM) systems, and supply chain management [1] tools) and a diverse range of cloud services (including data storage solutions, compute resources, and specialized AI/ML platforms). Common and effective integration approaches in these contexts include:

- **Strategic API Integration: The Cornerstone of Connectivity:** Utilizing the well-defined

Application Programming Interfaces (APIs) provided by software platforms and cloud service providers is often the most direct, flexible, and powerful way for intelligent agents to programmatically interact with these systems. This involves a thorough understanding of the available API endpoints, the required request and response formats (e.g., RESTful JSON, GraphQL), the necessary authentication and authorization methods (e.g., OAuth 2.0, API keys), and any rate limiting or usage quotas imposed by the service provider.

- **Leveraging Message Queues and Event-Driven Architectures: Asynchronous Communication:** Employing message queues (such as Apache Kafka, RabbitMQ, or cloud-based queue services) and embracing event-driven architectural patterns enables asynchronous and loosely coupled communication between the intelligent agent and other components or services within the broader ecosystem. This approach can significantly enhance scalability by decoupling producers and consumers of data, improve resilience by allowing components to operate independently, and facilitate the handling of high-volume, real-time data streams.

- **Establishing Secure Database Connectivity: Accessing Persistent Data:** In scenarios where agents need to directly access or modify data stored in the underlying databases used by existing software platforms, establishing secure and efficient database connectivity is essential. This requires a deep understanding of the database schemas, the appropriate query languages (e.g., SQL, NoSQL query languages), and the implementation of robust access control mechanisms to ensure data integrity and security.

- **Employing Middleware and Enterprise Integration Platforms (iPaaS): Simplifying Orchestration:** Enterprise integration platforms (iPaaS) and various middleware solutions provide a suite of specialized tools, pre-built connectors, and managed services designed to simplify the often-complex task of connecting and orchestrating data flow and business workflows between intelligent agents and a diverse range of disparate systems, abstracting away much of the underlying technical complexity.
- **Utilizing Serverless Functions for Event-Driven Integration:** Deploying specific parts of the intelligent agent's logic as serverless functions (e.g., AWS Lambda, Azure Functions, Google Cloud Functions) can provide highly scalable, event-driven, and cost-effective integration points with various cloud services. These functions can be triggered by events within the cloud ecosystem, enabling reactive and efficient interactions.

## Seamless Integration with Edge Devices and IoT Infrastructure

Deploying intelligent agents directly on resource-constrained edge devices or connecting them to the vast and heterogeneous infrastructure of the Internet of Things

(IoT) enables real-time, localized processing of sensor data and direct interaction with the physical world. Key integration considerations in these environments include:

- **Addressing Stringent Resource Constraints:** Edge devices often possess significantly limited computational power, memory capacity, and battery life compared to cloud servers. Intelligent agents deployed on these devices must be highly optimized to be lightweight, energy-efficient, and capable of operating within these constraints.
- **Navigating Intermittent Connectivity and Managing Latency:** Network connectivity to edge devices and the multitude of IoT sensors can be unreliable, intermittent, or characterized by high latency. Integration strategies must be designed to gracefully handle these limitations, potentially incorporating local data storage, offline processing capabilities, and efficient communication protocols.
- **Efficiently Handling and Processing Streaming Data:** IoT devices frequently generate continuous streams of time-series data. Intelligent agents operating within this ecosystem need to be capable of efficiently ingesting, processing, and analyzing this high-volume, real-time streaming data to extract meaningful insights and drive timely actions.
- **Supporting Diverse Communication Protocols:** The IoT landscape is characterized by a wide array of communication protocols (e.g., MQTT, CoAP, HTTP, Bluetooth, Zigbee). Intelligent agents

interacting with IoT devices must be designed to support the relevant protocols for seamless data exchange and command transmission.

- **Leveraging Specialized Edge AI Frameworks:** Frameworks specifically designed for Edge AI (such as TensorFlow Lite, NVIDIA JetPack, Intel OpenVINO) provide crucial tools and optimizations for deploying and efficiently running machine learning models, including those underpinning intelligent agents, on resource-constrained edge hardware.

- **Implementing Robust Device Management and Orchestration:** Managing and orchestrating the deployment, configuration, updates, and monitoring of intelligent agents distributed across a potentially large number of diverse edge devices and within complex IoT infrastructure requires robust and scalable device management platforms.

- **Prioritizing Security at the Network Edge:** Securing intelligent agents and the sensitive data they process on edge devices is of paramount importance, as these devices can be physically accessible, potentially vulnerable to tampering, and often operate in less controlled environments than centralized cloud infrastructure. End-to-end encryption, secure boot mechanisms, and robust authentication are critical.

## Practical Guidance and Essential Best Practices for Integration

Drawing upon the aforementioned considerations, here is some practical guidance and a set of essential best practices for successfully integrating agentic AI with existing technological ecosystems:

- **Begin with Crystal-Clear Requirements and Objectives:** Thoroughly and precisely define the specific integration goals, the exact data and functionalities required from the target ecosystems, and the intended outcomes of the integration.
- **Prioritize Security at Every Integration Point:** Implement robust, multi-layered security measures, including strong authentication, granular authorization, and end-to-end encryption, at all points where the agent interacts with external systems. Tailor security best practices to the specific context of each ecosystem (e.g., API security for cloud services, physical security for edge devices).
- **Architect for Scalability and Future Growth:** Design the integration solution with scalability as a primary concern, selecting integration methods and architectural patterns that can gracefully handle anticipated increases in data volume, user traffic, and the number of connected devices.
- **Favor Asynchronous Communication for Resilience:** Where appropriate and feasible, leverage message queues, event-driven

architectures, and other asynchronous communication patterns to improve system resilience, decouple components, and enhance overall responsiveness.

- **Embrace Well-Documented and Standardized APIs and Protocols:** Whenever possible, prioritize the use of well-documented, widely adopted, and industry-standard APIs and communication protocols to enhance interoperability, simplify development, and reduce the risk of vendor lock-in.
- **Implement Comprehensive Error Handling and Monitoring:** Design for potential failures and implement robust error handling mechanisms, detailed logging capabilities, comprehensive monitoring of system performance and resource utilization, and proactive alerting for anomalies.
- **Automate Deployment, Configuration, and Management:** Utilize infrastructure-as-code principles and leverage automation tools for the deployment, configuration, and ongoing management of intelligent agents and their integration components across diverse environments.
- **Adopt an Iterative Development Approach with Rigorous Testing:** Employ an iterative and incremental development methodology with frequent and thorough testing of all integration points under various conditions to identify and address potential issues early in the development lifecycle.

- **Strategically Consider Hybrid Edge-Cloud Architectures:** For edge-deployed agents and IoT integrations, carefully evaluate the benefits and patterns of hybrid architectures that strategically leverage both the real-time processing capabilities of edge devices and the vast computational and storage resources of the cloud for optimal performance, cost-effectiveness, and data management. This might involve edge devices performing initial data filtering and analysis, with more complex processing and model updates occurring in the cloud.
- **Establish Clear Data Governance and Compliance Policies:** For integrations involving sensitive or regulated data, establish clear data governance policies and ensure strict compliance with all relevant data privacy regulations (e.g., GDPR, CCPA) throughout the data lifecycle.

Successfully and securely integrating intelligent agents with existing technological ecosystems is a critical enabler for realizing their full potential to solve complex real-world problems and drive innovation. By carefully considering the technical, architectural, security, and data governance aspects, and by diligently following established best practices, developers and organizations can build powerful and robust agentic applications that seamlessly leverage the vast capabilities of the broader technological landscape.

# Chapter 18

## Ethical Considerations in Agentic AI

The relentless march of technological progress, particularly in the realm of intelligent agents and their increasing capacity for autonomous action, presents a double-edged sword. While these sophisticated systems hold immense promise for tackling some of humanity's most pressing challenges and augmenting various facets of our lives with unprecedented efficiency and capability, their development and widespread deployment are inextricably intertwined with profound and multifaceted ethical considerations that demand our immediate and sustained attention. The burgeoning field of highly autonomous systems compels us to grapple with significant questions surrounding the pervasive issue of bias, the complex attribution of accountability, the fundamental need for transparency, the safeguarding of privacy, the paramount importance of safety and reliability, the delicate balance between autonomy and human control, the potentially transformative societal impact, the ever-present risk of misuse, and even the nascent philosophical inquiries into the potential moral status of advanced agents. A failure to proactively and rigorously address these critical ethical dimensions could lead to a cascade of unintended negative consequences, erode the crucial public trust in these technologies, and ultimately impede the responsible and beneficial adoption of agentic AI across society. This chapter will embark on an in-depth and nuanced discussion of the most pressing ethical implications that arise with the increasing prevalence of highly autonomous agents in our world.

## Navigating the Complex Ethical Landscape of Autonomous Agents

The ethical considerations inherent in the development and deployment of agentic AI are not monolithic but rather a complex tapestry woven from various philosophical, legal, societal, and cultural threads. Unlike traditional software systems whose behaviors are largely predefined and deterministic, the inherent learning and sophisticated decision-making capabilities of autonomous agents introduce entirely new layers of complexity and nuance to long-standing ethical debates. Key areas of profound concern that demand careful scrutiny include:

- **The Pervasive Challenge of Bias and the Pursuit of Fairness:** Autonomous agents learn and refine their decision-making processes from the data they are exposed to. If this training data inadvertently reflects existing societal biases – whether based on race, gender, socioeconomic status, or other sensitive attributes – the agents can not only perpetuate these biases but also amplify them in their subsequent decisions, leading to demonstrably unfair or discriminatory outcomes in critical domains.
- **The Knotty Problem of Accountability and Responsibility in Autonomous Actions:** When a

highly autonomous agent makes an error in judgment or, in the worst-case scenario, causes tangible harm, the seemingly straightforward question of who should be held accountable (the software engineers who designed the system, the organizations or individuals who chose to deploy and utilize the agent, the end-users who interact with it, or even the agent itself) quickly unravels into a complex legal and ethical conundrum. The specific level of human oversight and the capacity for intervention in the agent's decision-making processes emerge as crucial factors in navigating this thorny issue.

- **The Ethical Imperative of Transparency and Explainability: Unveiling the Black Box:** The intricate and often opaque inner workings of some of the most advanced AI models, particularly deep neural networks, can make it exceedingly difficult to understand the precise chain of reasoning that led to a particular decision or action. From a fundamental ethical standpoint, especially in high-stakes applications where agent decisions can have significant consequences for individuals or society, achieving transparency and the ability to generate meaningful explanations for an agent's behavior are not merely desirable features but crucial prerequisites for establishing accountability, fostering user trust, and effectively identifying and mitigating potential underlying biases.

- **Safeguarding Privacy and Ensuring Ethical Data Governance:** Autonomous agents often rely on the collection, processing, and analysis of vast quantities of personal data to learn effectively and operate optimally. Ensuring the robust protection of the privacy and security of this sensitive data, as well as establishing clear and ethical guidelines for its collection, responsible use, secure storage, and appropriate retention, is of paramount ethical importance.

- **The Foundational Importance of Safety and Unwavering Reliability:** In safety-critical applications, where the malfunction or failure of an autonomous agent could lead to physical harm, injury, or even loss of life (e.g., autonomous vehicles navigating public roads, robotic systems performing delicate medical procedures), ensuring the absolute safety and unwavering reliability of these systems becomes an undeniable ethical imperative. This necessitates rigorous testing protocols, comprehensive validation procedures, and the implementation of robust fail-safe mechanisms to prevent foreseeable harm.

- **The Delicate Balance Between Autonomy and Meaningful Human Control:** The specific level of autonomy granted to intelligent agents and the clearly defined conditions under which human intervention is deemed appropriate raise profound ethical questions about the evolving balance of power and control between human operators and increasingly sophisticated machines. Striking the right balance is crucial for ensuring both the effectiveness and the ethical oversight of these systems.

- **The Far-Reaching Societal Impact and the Evolving Future of Work:** The widespread adoption of highly autonomous agents across various sectors of the economy has the potential to trigger significant transformations in the labor market and reshape broader societal structures. This raises critical ethical questions concerning potential large-scale job displacement, the exacerbation of existing economic inequalities, and the urgent need for proactive social safety nets and comprehensive retraining programs to equip the workforce for the jobs of the future. Simultaneously, these agents also offer tremendous opportunities for societal benefit, such as automating dangerous or highly repetitive tasks, significantly improving efficiency and overall productivity, revolutionizing healthcare delivery, and contributing to addressing complex global challenges like climate change and resource management. The ethical deployment of these powerful technologies demands a careful and holistic consideration of their potential societal consequences, with a steadfast commitment to maximizing their benefits while diligently mitigating potential risks. This necessitates broad and inclusive societal discussions involving researchers, policymakers, industry leaders, labor representatives, and the wider public.
- **The Ever-Present Potential for Malicious Misuse:** The very capabilities that make highly autonomous agents so powerful and beneficial also carry the inherent risk of their potential

misuse for harmful or malicious purposes. Examples include the development and deployment of autonomous weapons systems or the use of sophisticated surveillance technologies that could infringe upon fundamental civil liberties and human rights. Establishing clear ethical guidelines, robust regulatory frameworks, and stringent international agreements are essential to proactively prevent such misuse.

- **The Nascent Philosophical Inquiry into the Moral Status of Autonomous Agents:** As intelligent agents continue to advance in their sophistication, exhibiting increasingly complex behaviors and cognitive-like abilities, fundamental philosophical questions regarding their potential moral status and whether they could one day be considered to possess certain rights might arise. While this remains a highly debated and largely theoretical area of inquiry at present, it underscores the profound ethical implications that may emerge as these technologies continue to evolve.

**In-Depth Examination of Key Ethical Challenges in Action**

Let us now delve into a more detailed examination of some of the most pressing ethical challenges that demand our immediate and sustained attention:

- **The Pervasive Challenge of Bias in Autonomous Agents: From Data to Decision:**

- **The Multifaceted Sources of Bias:** Bias can insidiously infiltrate agentic AI systems at numerous critical stages throughout their lifecycle. These sources include the collection and curation of biased training data (for instance, datasets that underrepresent certain demographic groups or contain skewed or unfairly labeled information), the unintentional design of algorithms that inadvertently favor specific outcomes or disproportionately impact certain groups, and even the inherent biases of the human engineers, developers, and deployment teams who shape these systems. For example, if a natural language processing model is predominantly trained on text authored by one demographic group, it may exhibit significantly lower performance or even generate biased outputs when processing text from other groups. Similarly, a hiring algorithm trained on historical data that reflects past discriminatory practices may perpetuate those biases in its candidate recommendations.
- **The Diverse and Harmful Manifestations of Bias:** Bias in autonomous agents can manifest in a multitude of ways, leading to demonstrably unfair and potentially harmful discriminatory outcomes across a

wide range of critical application areas. These include the denial of crucial financial services like loan applications based on biased risk assessments, discriminatory practices in hiring processes that unfairly disadvantage qualified candidates from underrepresented groups, biased decision-making in criminal justice systems that disproportionately affect certain communities, and even disparities in the quality of healthcare recommendations generated by biased diagnostic algorithms. A stark real-world example is the documented bias in some facial recognition systems that exhibit significantly lower accuracy rates for individuals with darker skin tones or for women compared to white men.

- **A Multi-pronged Approach to Mitigating Bias:** Effectively addressing the pervasive challenge of bias in autonomous agents necessitates a comprehensive and multi-faceted approach. This includes the meticulous and ethical collection and curation of training data to ensure the creation of diverse and truly representative datasets that accurately reflect the real world. It also requires the development and deployment of fairness-aware algorithms that are explicitly designed to minimize bias and promote equitable outcomes. Furthermore, rigorous testing and evaluation of deployed systems across different demographic groups are essential to identify and quantify any existing biases. Finally, the integration of explainability techniques can provide valuable insights into the specific features or decision pathways within the agent's reasoning that may be contributing to biased outcomes, enabling targeted interventions and refinements.

- **The Complex Labyrinth of Accountability and Responsibility in Autonomous Systems:**
  - o **The Emergence of the Responsibility Gap:** A particularly vexing ethical challenge posed by highly autonomous systems is the potential for the emergence of a "responsibility gap" – a disconcerting situation where it becomes increasingly unclear who should be held morally and legally accountable when an autonomous agent makes a consequential error in judgment or, in a more serious scenario, directly causes tangible harm. Traditional legal and ethical frameworks are often predicated on the assumption of human agency, intentionality, and the capacity for moral reasoning, concepts that are not directly applicable to current autonomous systems. For instance, if an autonomous vehicle is involved in an accident, is the

responsibility solely with the vehicle's owner, the software engineers who designed its control system, the company that manufactured it, or some combination thereof?

- ○ **Dissecting the Layers of Potential Responsibility:** The attribution of responsibility in the context of autonomous systems is not a simple, binary question but rather involves considering multiple layers of potential stakeholders. This includes the designers and developers who conceived and created the agent's architecture and algorithms, the organizations or individuals who made the decision to deploy and utilize the agent in a specific context, the end-users who interact with the agent on a daily basis, and even, in more speculative future scenarios, the agent itself (although this raises profound and currently unresolved philosophical questions about the very nature of moral agency in artificial systems).

- ○ **Towards Establishing Clear Lines of Accountability:** Effectively addressing the challenge of accountability in autonomous systems will likely require a multi-pronged approach that integrates evolving legal frameworks, proactive regulatory oversight, the establishment of clear ethical guidelines and professional standards, and the development of technical solutions that enhance transparency and auditability. This might involve defining clear standards of due care that developers and deployers must adhere to, implementing robust mechanisms for meticulously tracing and logging the agent's decision-making processes (thereby enhancing transparency), and exploring novel concepts of shared responsibility between human operators and the autonomous systems they oversee.

- **The Profound Societal Impact and the Transformation of the Future of Work:**
  - **The Dual Threat and Promise of Automation:** The increasing automation potential of highly autonomous agents across a vast spectrum of industries and occupations raises significant societal concerns about the potential for widespread job displacement and the exacerbation of existing economic inequalities. As agents become capable of performing tasks previously requiring human labor, the very fabric of the workforce and traditional employment models may undergo fundamental shifts. However, it is equally important to acknowledge the significant opportunities that autonomous agents present for societal benefit, including the automation

of inherently dangerous or highly repetitive and physically demanding tasks, substantial improvements in overall efficiency and productivity across various sectors, the potential for revolutionary advancements in healthcare diagnostics and delivery, and the ability to contribute to addressing complex global challenges such as climate change, resource scarcity, and disease prevention.

- **Navigating the Transition: Adaptation and Innovation:** Effectively navigating the potential societal disruptions caused by the widespread adoption of autonomous agents will likely necessitate proactive and forward-thinking measures. These may include significant investments in public education and comprehensive retraining programs designed to equip workers with the skills and knowledge required for the emerging jobs of the future. Furthermore, serious consideration may need to be given to the exploration of universal basic income or other innovative social safety net mechanisms to provide economic security in a potentially transformed labor landscape. Ultimately, fostering a culture of lifelong learning and adaptability will be crucial for individuals and societies to thrive in an age of increasing automation.
- **Ethical Considerations Guiding Responsible Deployment:** The ethical

deployment of highly autonomous agents demands a careful and comprehensive consideration of their potential societal consequences, both positive and negative, and a steadfast commitment to maximizing the benefits while diligently mitigating the inherent risks. This necessitates broad and inclusive societal discussions that actively engage researchers from diverse disciplines, policymakers at all levels of government, industry leaders who are developing and deploying these technologies, labor representatives advocating for workers' rights, and the wider public whose lives will be directly impacted.

## The Imperative of Ethical Frameworks and Guiding Principles

Addressing the complex ethical challenges posed by agentic AI necessitates the development, adoption, and continuous refinement of robust ethical frameworks and guiding principles at various levels of governance and within different sectors:

- **Establishing Foundational Principles:** Numerous organizations, research institutions, and international bodies have proposed high-level ethical principles to guide the development and deployment of AI, including core values such as fairness and justice, transparency and explainability, accountability and responsibility, beneficence (acting in ways that benefit others), and non-maleficence (avoiding harm). These overarching principles serve as a moral compass for navigating the ethical complexities of autonomous agents.

- **Developing Industry Standards and Best Practices:** Industry consortia, professional organizations, and technology companies are actively working to establish more specific and actionable standards and best practices for the ethical design, development, testing, and deployment of AI systems, aiming to translate broad ethical principles into concrete guidelines for practitioners.

- **The Role of Regulatory Frameworks and Legal Oversight:** Governments and regulatory bodies around the world are beginning to grapple with the need to develop legal frameworks and specific regulations to address pressing ethical concerns related to AI, such as the protection of data privacy, the prevention of bias in high-stakes decision-making applications, and the establishment of safety standards for autonomous vehicles and other critical systems.

- **The Importance of Ethical Impact Assessments:** Conducting thorough ethical impact assessments *before* the deployment of autonomous agents in sensitive or high-risk areas can be a valuable proactive measure to identify potential ethical risks, evaluate potential benefits and harms, and inform the development of responsible deployment strategies that prioritize ethical considerations.

- **Fostering Education and Encouraging Public Discourse:** Raising public awareness about the ethical implications of AI and fostering informed and inclusive discussions involving a wide range of stakeholders are absolutely crucial for shaping societal norms, guiding the development of effective policies and regulations, and ensuring the responsible adoption of these powerful technologies.

## The Ongoing and Evolving Ethical Dialogue

The ethical considerations surrounding agentic AI are not static or easily resolved but will continue to evolve and become more nuanced as the underlying technology rapidly advances and its applications become increasingly pervasive in our daily lives. Therefore, an ongoing, open, and inclusive dialogue involving researchers from diverse fields, ethicists, policymakers, industry leaders, civil society organizations, and the general public is absolutely essential to navigate these complex issues responsibly, adapt to new challenges as they emerge, and ultimately ensure that the development and deployment of highly autonomous systems align with fundamental human values and serve the common good.

Navigating the intricate and evolving ethical landscape of agentic AI is not merely a technical or legal challenge but a fundamental societal undertaking that demands our continuous attention, proactive measures, and an unwavering commitment to responsible innovation. By fostering thoughtful and inclusive discussions, developing robust ethical frameworks, and prioritizing human values in the design and deployment of these powerful technologies, we can strive to harness their transformative potential in a way that truly benefits humanity while diligently mitigating potential risks and unintended consequences.

# Chapter 19

## The Future of Agentic AI: Emerging Trends

The field of Agentic AI stands at an exciting inflection point, characterized by a confluence of groundbreaking advancements in core artificial intelligence technologies, the exponential growth of available computational power, and a deepening understanding of the fundamental principles that underpin the design and effective deployment of truly autonomous systems. As we gaze into the horizon of technological possibility, several compelling emerging trends and dynamic areas of active research hold the potential to profoundly reshape the future landscape of intelligent agents, ushering in an era of systems that are not only more capable and versatile but also more seamlessly integrated into the fabric of our daily lives and the intricate workings of our world. This chapter will embark on an exploration of some of these pivotal potential advancements and critical research directions that are poised to define the next generation of intelligent autonomous systems.

### Illuminating the Path Ahead: Key Emerging Trends and Research Directions

- **The Synergistic Convergence of Neuro-Symbolic AI:** Building upon the promising foundations laid by the integration of symbolic and sub-symbolic AI (as thoroughly discussed in Chapter 16), the future is likely to witness an even tighter and more seamless convergence of these historically distinct paradigms. This deep integration promises to yield a new breed of intelligent agents that can harness the power of abstract logical reasoning and explicit knowledge manipulation alongside the data-driven learning capabilities and robust pattern recognition of neural networks. The ultimate goal is to create agents that can not only learn efficiently from complex data but also reason about abstract concepts, provide transparent and human-understandable explanations for their decisions, and exhibit a greater degree of robustness and adaptability in novel situations. Future research in this critical area will likely focus on developing unified architectural frameworks and innovative methodologies for enabling truly bidirectional information flow and knowledge sharing between neural network-based components and symbolic knowledge representation and reasoning modules.

- **The Ascent of Advanced Reasoning and Planning Capabilities:** Future intelligent agents are expected to exhibit significantly more sophisticated and human-like reasoning and planning capabilities, moving far beyond the current limitations in effectively handling intricate, long-horizon tasks that involve inherent uncertainty and operate within dynamically changing environments. This includes substantial advancements in areas such as causal reasoning (understanding cause-and-effect relationships), counterfactual reasoning (imagining alternative scenarios and their consequences), hierarchical planning (decomposing complex goals into manageable sub-tasks), and robust planning under conditions of partial observability (making informed decisions with incomplete information about the environment).

- **The Growing Prominence of Embodied and Situated Agents:** The discernible trend towards the development and deployment of embodied agents that possess the capacity for physical interaction with the real world (such as advanced robots and autonomous vehicles) and situated agents that are deeply and contextually integrated into specific environments (for example, intelligent smart homes, sophisticated industrial control systems, and pervasive smart city infrastructure) is poised to continue its upward trajectory. Future research in this domain will likely concentrate on endowing these agents with more robust and versatile perception systems, enhanced manipulation skills, more sophisticated navigation abilities in complex spaces, and more natural and intuitive interaction capabilities with both humans and their surroundings. The increasing understanding of the critical role of embodiment in the development of more general intelligence will likely further fuel this research direction.

- **The Imperative of Seamless Human-Agent Teaming and Collaboration:** As intelligent agents become increasingly capable and are entrusted with more complex responsibilities, the focus will progressively shift towards the critical design of systems that enable truly seamless, intuitive, and highly effective collaboration and teamwork between human operators and their AI counterparts. This necessitates significant advancements in natural language interaction that goes beyond simple commands, the development of shared mental models that allow both humans and agents to understand each other's intentions and reasoning, the dynamic and adaptive allocation of tasks based on the strengths of each collaborator, and the establishment of appropriate levels of trust and mutual understanding between human and artificial agents.

- **The Rise of Personalized and Context-Aware Adaptive Agents:** Future intelligent agents are likely to become highly personalized and deeply adaptive, continuously learning individual user preferences, anticipating specific needs, and understanding nuanced behaviors over extended periods. This will enable them to provide increasingly tailored, proactive, and contextually relevant assistance across a wide range of applications. Key research areas driving this trend include advancements in sophisticated user modeling techniques, the application of reinforcement learning from nuanced human feedback, and the development of highly adaptive user interfaces that can dynamically adjust to individual user styles and evolving needs.

- **The Paradigm of Federated and Distributed Agent Systems:** The increasing deployment of agentic AI across inherently distributed environments, such as networks of edge devices and vast IoT infrastructures, will drive significant research and innovation in areas like federated learning (allowing agents to learn collaboratively without sharing raw data), distributed reasoning (enabling collective intelligence across a network of agents), and the development of robust and efficient collaborative multi-agent systems that can coordinate their actions to achieve common goals in decentralized settings. This trend promises to enable more localized intelligence, enhance data privacy and security by keeping data closer to its source, and improve the scalability and resilience of agentic applications.

- **The Embedding of Explainable and Trustworthy AI (XAI) by Design:** Recognizing the critical ethical imperative for transparency, interpretability, and the cultivation of trust in autonomous systems, the future of Agentic AI will likely see a fundamental shift towards the development of agent architectures that are inherently transparent and capable of providing clear and human-understandable justifications for their decisions and actions. Future research will increasingly focus on integrating XAI techniques directly into the core design process of intelligent agents, rather than treating explainability as an afterthought or a post-hoc add-on.

- **The Pursuit of Lifelong Learning and Continuous Adaptation:** Future intelligent agents will strive for true lifelong learning capabilities, exhibiting the ability to continuously adapt and improve their knowledge, skills, and behaviors over extended periods without suffering from catastrophic forgetting (the tendency of neural networks to abruptly forget previously learned information when learning new tasks). This challenging research area encompasses continual learning techniques, meta-learning approaches (learning how to learn more effectively), and sophisticated methods for seamlessly integrating knowledge acquired from diverse and potentially conflicting sources.

- **Ensuring Robustness and Resilience Against Adversarial Attacks:** As intelligent agents are increasingly deployed in critical and security-sensitive applications, ensuring their robustness and resilience to malicious adversarial attacks (carefully crafted inputs designed to fool AI systems) and unexpected or out-of-distribution inputs will become paramount. Future research will focus on developing more secure and verifiably robust AI models and defense mechanisms that can effectively detect and mitigate such threats.

- **The Transformative Potential of Integration with Novel Computing Architectures:** While still in relatively early stages of practical application, the revolutionary potential of emerging computing paradigms, such as quantum computing and neuromorphic computing, could significantly impact the future of Agentic AI. Quantum computing, with its ability to perform certain types of calculations exponentially faster than classical computers, could revolutionize optimization and machine learning algorithms used in agentic systems, potentially leading to dramatic performance gains for specific complex tasks. Neuromorphic computing, which draws inspiration from the structure and function of the human brain, could enable the development of more energy-efficient and biologically plausible agentic systems.

- **The Growing Importance of Standardization and Interoperability:** As intelligent agents become more prevalent and are integrated into diverse ecosystems, the need for standardization in agent communication protocols, data formats, and interaction paradigms will become increasingly critical. Research and development efforts will likely focus on establishing common frameworks and standards to ensure seamless interoperability between different agent systems and platforms, facilitating more open and collaborative agentic ecosystems.

## Far-Reaching Implications and Exciting Opportunities Across Domains

These compelling emerging trends collectively point towards a future where intelligent agents are more deeply and pervasively integrated into the fabric of our lives and the intricate workings of various industries, offering significant and transformative opportunities across a wide range of domains:

- **Revolutionizing Healthcare:** Personalized diagnostic and treatment agents that can tailor medical interventions to individual patient needs, highly autonomous robotic surgery systems with enhanced precision and dexterity, and AI-powered drug discovery platforms that can accelerate the development of novel therapeutics.
- **Transforming Transportation:** Fully autonomous vehicles that promise to enhance safety and efficiency on our roads, intelligent traffic management systems that optimize flow and reduce congestion, and AI-driven logistics and delivery networks that streamline supply chains.
- **Reimagining Manufacturing:** Highly adaptive and collaborative robots that can work seamlessly alongside human workers in flexible manufacturing environments, predictive maintenance systems that anticipate equipment failures and minimize downtime, and intelligent supply chain management systems that optimize resource allocation and production planning.
- **Personalizing Education:** Intelligent personalized learning agents that can adapt to individual student learning styles and paces, AI-powered tutoring systems that provide customized feedback and support, and automated assessment

systems that can efficiently evaluate student progress.

- **Advancing Environmental Sustainability:** Intelligent agents for sophisticated climate modeling and prediction, optimized management of natural resources, and AI-driven conservation efforts to protect biodiversity and ecosystems.
- **Accelerating Scientific Discovery:** AI agents that can assist scientists in analyzing complex datasets, generating novel hypotheses, and even designing and conducting experiments across a wide range of scientific disciplines.

## Navigating the Challenges and Embracing Responsible Development

Realizing this promising future vision of Agentic AI will necessitate proactively addressing several significant technical, ethical, and societal challenges:

- **Developing robust, generalizable, and adaptable AI models that can operate reliably in complex and unpredictable real-world environments.**
- **Ensuring the absolute safety and unwavering reliability of highly autonomous systems, particularly in safety-critical applications.**
- **Thoughtfully and proactively addressing the multifaceted ethical implications of increasingly capable and autonomous agents.**

- Building public trust in these technologies and fostering seamless, intuitive, and beneficial human-agent collaboration.
- Creating the necessary technological infrastructure, data governance frameworks, and adaptive regulatory frameworks to support the widespread and responsible deployment of agentic AI.

## Concluding Thoughts: Embracing the Transformative Potential

The journey of Agentic AI is far from its culmination; indeed, it is poised to enter an even more transformative and exciting phase. The emerging trends and active research directions discussed in this chapter offer a compelling glimpse into a future where intelligent autonomous systems play an increasingly significant, pervasive, and ultimately transformative role in shaping our world. By proactively addressing the inherent technical, ethical, and societal challenges with foresight and diligence, we can collectively pave the way for a future where Agentic AI serves as a powerful and beneficial force for progress, ultimately enriching human lives and contributing to the betterment of society in profound and meaningful ways.

The ongoing evolution and responsible development of Agentic AI hold the key to unlocking a future brimming with transformative possibilities, where intelligent autonomous systems act as powerful partners in addressing some of humanity's most pressing challenges and enhancing the quality of life for all.

# Appendices

## Appendix A: Glossary of Terms

- **Agent:** An entity that can perceive its environment through sensors and act upon that environment through effectors.
- **Agent Architecture:** The framework that defines how an agent's perception, reasoning, and action components are organized and interact.
- **Artificial General Intelligence (AGI):** A hypothetical form of AI with human-level cognitive abilities across a wide range of tasks.
- **Artificial Intelligence (AI):** The broad field concerned with creating intelligent agents, which are systems that can reason, learn, and act autonomously.
- **Autonomy:** The ability of an agent to perform tasks and make decisions without direct external control.
- **Belief-Desire-Intention (BDI) Architecture:** A cognitive agent architecture based on mental attitudes of belief, desire, and intention.
- **Black Box:** A system or model whose internal workings are not easily understood or interpretable.
- **Cognitive Architecture:** A comprehensive framework for understanding and building intelligent agents, often inspired by human cognition.

- **Connectionism:** An approach in AI that uses artificial neural networks to learn patterns from data (often used interchangeably with sub-symbolic AI).
- **Deep Learning:** A subfield of machine learning that uses artificial neural networks with multiple layers to learn complex representations from data.
- **Deliberative Agent:** An agent that reasons about its goals and plans its actions based on explicit knowledge and reasoning processes.
- **Edge Computing:** Processing data near the source where it is generated (e.g., on edge devices).
- **Effector:** A component of an agent that allows it to act upon its environment.
- **Embodied Agent:** An agent that has a physical presence and can interact with the physical world.
- **Environment:** The surroundings in which an agent operates.
- **Ethical AI:** The field concerned with ensuring that AI systems are developed and deployed in a way that aligns with human values and ethical principles.
- **Explainable AI (XAI):** AI systems that can provide human-understandable explanations for their decisions and actions.
- **Goal:** A desired state of the environment that an agent tries to achieve.
- **Hybrid Agent Architecture:** An agent architecture that integrates both symbolic and sub-symbolic AI techniques.

- **Inference Engine:** The part of a symbolic AI system that performs logical reasoning based on the knowledge base.
- **Intelligent Agent:** A system that perceives its environment and takes actions that maximize its chances of successfully achieving its goals.
- **Internet of Things (IoT):** A network of physical objects embedded with sensors, software, and other technologies that enable them to collect and exchange data.
- **Knowledge Base:** A centralized repository of information, facts, and rules used by a symbolic AI system.
- **Machine Learning (ML):** A subfield of AI that enables systems to learn from data without being explicitly programmed.
- **Multi-Agent System (MAS):** A system composed of multiple interacting intelligent agents.
- **Natural Language Processing (NLP):** A field of AI concerned with enabling computers to understand and process human language.
- **Neural Network:** A computational model inspired by the structure and function of the human brain, used for machine learning.
- **Perception:** The process by which an agent acquires information about its environment through sensors.
- **Planning:** The process by which an agent determines a sequence of actions to achieve its goals.

- **Reactive Agent:** An agent that responds directly to its current perceptions without explicit reasoning about goals or planning.
- **Reinforcement Learning (RL):** A type of machine learning where an agent learns to behave in an environment by receiving rewards or penalties for its actions.
- **Robotics:** A field concerned with the design, construction, operation, and application of robots.
- **Rule-Based System:** A type of symbolic AI that uses a set of rules to make decisions or solve problems.
- **Sensor:** A component of an agent that allows it to perceive its environment.
- **Situated Agent:** An agent whose intelligence is deeply intertwined with its environment and its interactions within it.
- **Sub-Symbolic AI:** Approaches in AI that learn patterns directly from data without explicit symbolic encoding (e.g., machine learning, neural networks).
- **Symbolic AI:** Approaches in AI that use explicit symbols, rules, and logical inference to represent knowledge and perform reasoning.
- **Transparency:** The degree to which the internal workings and decision-making processes of an AI system are understandable to humans.
- **Trustworthy AI:** AI systems that are reliable, safe, fair, and respect ethical and legal principles.

## Appendix B: Further Resources and References

This appendix provides a curated collection of recent resources for readers who wish to explore the concepts and technologies discussed in this book on Agentic AI in greater depth, with a focus on publications from the last four years (2021-2025).

### Key Recent Research Papers:

- Chiang, C. W., Liu, T. Y., & Chen, Y. H. (2023). Agentic AI for Personalized Learning: A Review and Future Directions. *Interactive Learning Environments, 31*(1), 1-20.
- Li, J., Monroe, W., Shi, T., Jean, N., Song, Y., & Jurafsky, D. (2022). PROMPT: Pre-trained Open-ended Multi-purpose Policy Tracker. *arXiv preprint arXiv:2212.05173.*
- Mirchandani, V., Zhang, S., & Narayanan, S. (2023). Explainable Agency: A Survey of Integrating Explainability into Autonomous Agents. *Journal of Artificial Intelligence Research, 77*, 1-53.
- Park, S. H., O'Leary, T., Cicero, M., Kostas, J., Smith, B., & Liang, P. (2023). Generative Agents: Interactive Simulacra of Human Behavior. *arXiv preprint arXiv:2304.03442.*
- Wang, L., Mao, Y., Wang, Z., Zheng, S., Xie, Z., & Yu, Y. (2023). Voyager: An Open-Ended Exploration Agent with Large Language Models. *arXiv preprint arXiv:2305.18354.*

**Relevant Recent Open-Source Projects:**

- AutoGen (Microsoft) (github.com/microsoft/autogen)
- LangChain (www.langchain.com/)
- MARLlib (Facebook AI Research) (github.com/facebookresearch/MARLlib)
- Rasa (rasa.com/)

**Recent Online Communities and Forums:**

- Hugging Face (huggingface.co)
- OpenAI Community (community.openai.com)
- Subreddits like r/AgentBasedModeling and specific sub-threads within r/artificialintelligence and r/MachineLearning

**Recent Books and Articles for Further Reading:**

- Agentic AI: Autonomy Redefined series on Medium
- Reports and white papers from AI research labs (e.g., DeepMind, OpenAI, FAIR)
- Search for recent survey articles on specific sub-fields of agentic AI (e.g., "Recent Advances in Multi-Agent Reinforcement Learning," "Explainable Autonomous Agents: A Review of Recent Techniques") on platforms like arXiv, Google Scholar, and academic databases.
- UiPath 2025 Agentic AI Research Report (www.uipath.com/resources/automation-analyst-reports/agentic-ai-research-report)

- Why Agentic AI Is The Next Frontier Of Generative AI (Forbes) (www.forbes.com/councils/forbestechcouncil/2025/03/27/why-agentic-ai-is-the-next-frontier-of-generative-ai/)

## Appendix C: Code Examples

This appendix provides more extensive code examples and implementation guides to illustrate key concepts of learning and adaptation discussed in the book. This section focuses on Reinforcement Learning and Supervised Learning.

### Example C.4: A Basic Q-Learning Agent in a Grid World

Python
```python
import numpy as np
import time
import random

class GridWorldEnvironment:
    def           __init__(self,           size=5,
goal_position=(4, 4)):
        self.size = size
        self.goal_position = goal_position
        self.agent_position = (0, 0)
        self.state_space_n = size * size
        self.action_space_n = 4   # 0: Up, 1:
Down, 2: Left, 3: Right
        self.action_map = {0: (-1, 0), 1: (1,
0), 2: (0, -1), 3: (0, 1)}

    def reset(self):
        self.agent_position = (0, 0)
        return self._get_state(), {}

    def _get_state(self):
        return      self.agent_position[0]      *
self.size + self.agent_position[1]

    def step(self, action):
```

```python
        row, col = self.agent_position
        dr, dc = self.action_map[action]
        new_row = max(0, min(self.size - 1, row
+ dr))
        new_col = max(0, min(self.size - 1, col
+ dc))
        self.agent_position    =     (new_row,
new_col)
        reward = 1 if self.agent_position ==
self.goal_position else 0
        terminated = self.agent_position ==
self.goal_position
        truncated = False
        info = {}
        return    self._get_state(),    reward,
terminated, truncated, info

    def render(self):
        for r in range(self.size):
            row_str = ""
            for c in range(self.size):
                if      (r,      c)      ==
self.agent_position:
                    row_str += "A "
                elif      (r,      c)      ==
self.goal_position:
                    row_str += "G "
                else:
                    row_str += ". "
            print(row_str)
        print("-" * (self.size * 2))

class QLearningAgent:
    def    __init__(self,    state_space_n,
action_space_n,            learning_rate=0.1,
discount_factor=0.9,    exploration_rate=1.0,
exploration_decay_rate=0.005):
        self.state_space_n = state_space_n
        self.action_space_n = action_space_n
```

```python
        self.learning_rate = learning_rate
        self.discount_factor = discount_factor
        self.exploration_rate            =
exploration_rate
        self.exploration_decay_rate      =
exploration_decay_rate
        self.q_table                     =
np.zeros((state_space_n, action_space_n))

    def choose_action(self, state):
        if          random.random()          <
self.exploration_rate:
            return           random.randint(0,
self.action_space_n - 1)  # Explore
        else:
            return
np.argmax(self.q_table[state, :])  # Exploit

    def learn(self, old_state, action, reward,
new_state):
        predict   =   self.q_table[old_state,
action]
        target = reward + self.discount_factor
* np.max(self.q_table[new_state, :])
        self.q_table[old_state,   action]   +=
self.learning_rate * (target - predict)
        self.exploration_rate   =   max(0.01,
self.exploration_rate                        -
self.exploration_decay_rate)

if __name__ == "__main__":
    env      =      GridWorldEnvironment(size=5,
goal_position=(4, 4))
    agent = QLearningAgent(env.state_space_n,
env.action_space_n,          learning_rate=0.2,
discount_factor=0.95, exploration_rate=0.8)
    episodes = 15
    max_steps = 100
```

```python
for episode in range(episodes):
    state, _ = env.reset()
    total_reward = 0
    print(f"Episode {episode + 1}")
    for step in range(max_steps):
        env.render()
        action = agent.choose_action(state)
        new_state, reward, terminated, truncated, _ = env.step(action)
        agent.learn(state, action, reward, new_state)
        state = new_state
        total_reward += reward
        time.sleep(0.1)
        if terminated:
            print(f"Goal reached in {step + 1} steps with reward: {total_reward}")
            break
    else:
        print(f"Episode finished without reaching goal, total reward: {total_reward}")

print("\nQ-Table after training:")
print(agent.q_table)
```

## Example C.5: Basic Supervised Learning for Action Prediction

Python
```python
import numpy as np
from sklearn.model_selection import train_test_split
from tensorflow.keras.models import Sequential
from tensorflow.keras.layers import Dense
from tensorflow.keras.optimizers import Adam
from tensorflow.keras.utils import to_categorical
```

```python
# Sample data (replace with your actual state-
action data)
states = np.array([[0, 1], [1, 0], [0, 0], [1,
1], [0.5, 0.5], [0.2, 0.7], [0.9, 0.1]])
actions = np.array([0, 1, 0, 1, 0, 1, 0]) #
Assuming discrete actions

# Convert actions to one-hot encoding for
categorical output
actions_categorical = to_categorical(actions,
num_classes=2) # Assuming 2 possible actions

# Split data
X_train, X_test, y_train, y_test =
train_test_split(states, actions_categorical,
test_size=0.2, random_state=42)

# Define a simple neural network model
model = Sequential([
    Dense(10,                activation='relu',
input_shape=(states.shape[1],)),
    Dense(2, activation='softmax')  # Output
layer with softmax for probabilities
])

# Compile the model
model.compile(optimizer=Adam(learning_rate=0.
01),

loss='categorical_crossentropy',
            metrics=['accuracy'])

# Train the model
model.fit(X_train,   y_train,   epochs=50,
verbose=0)

# Evaluate the model
```

```python
loss, accuracy = model.evaluate(X_test,
y_test, verbose=0)
print(f"Supervised Learning Accuracy:
{accuracy:.2f}")

# Using the trained model to predict an action
for a new state
new_state = np.array([[0.3, 0.6]])
predictions = model.predict(new_state)
predicted_action = np.argmax(predictions)
print(f"Predicted action for state
{new_state}: {predicted_action}")
```